W9-CHO-852

Christmas
2014

What is man that You take thought of him, and the son of man that You care for him?

PSALM 8:4 NASB

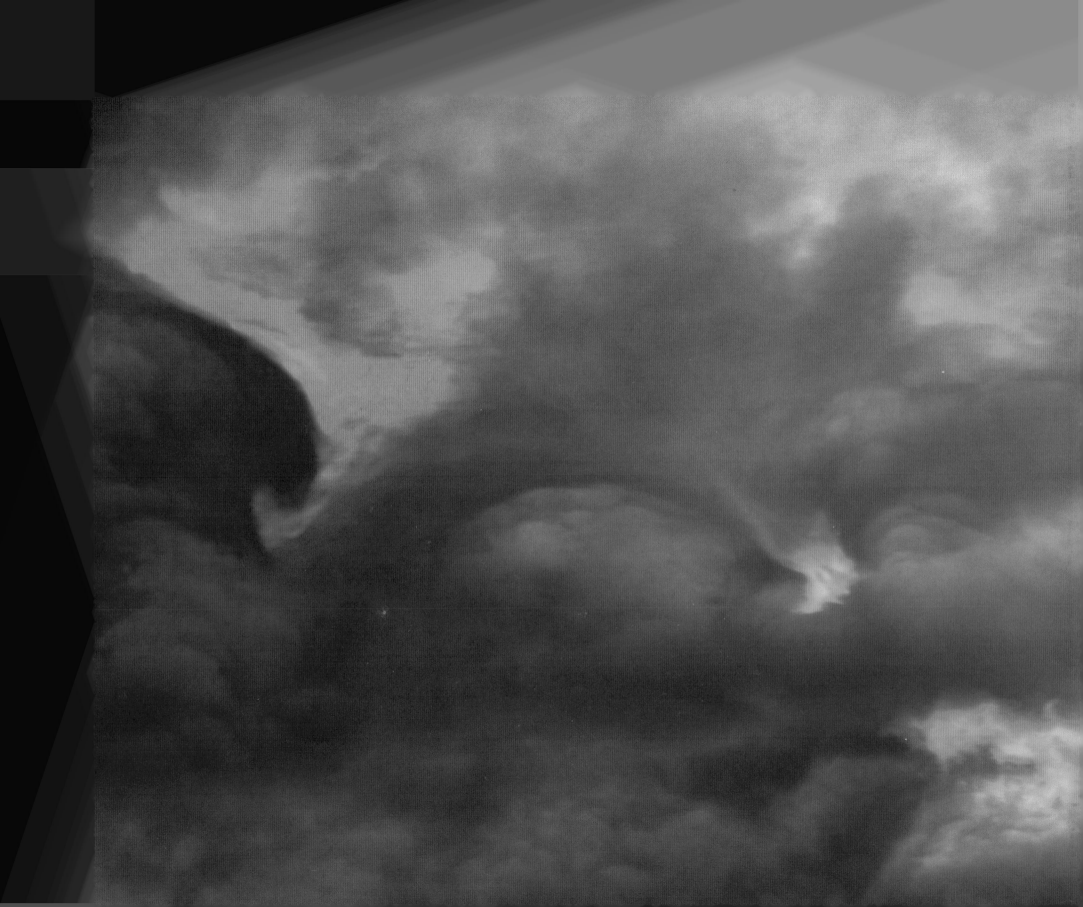

In the beginning God created the heavens and the earth. The earth was without form, and void; and darkness was on the face of the deep. And the Spirit of God was hovering over the face of the waters.

Then God said, "Let there be light"; and there was light. And God saw the light, that it was good; and God divided the light from the darkness. God called the light Day, and the darkness He called Night. So the evening and the morning were the first day.

GENESIS 1:1-5

2. Sunset, Ligurian Coast, Italy

Then God said, "Let there be a firmament in the midst of the waters, and let it divide the waters from the waters." Thus God made the firmament, and divided the waters which were under the firmament from the waters which were above the firmament; and it was so. And God called the firmament Heaven. So the evening and the morning were the second day.

GENESIS 1:6-8

Then God said, "Let the waters under the heavens be gathered together into one place, and let the dry land appear"; and it was so. And God called the dry land Earth, and the gathering together of the waters He called Seas. And God saw that it was good.

Then God said, "Let the earth bring forth grass, the herb that yields seed, and the fruit tree that yields fruit according to its kind, whose seed is in itself, on the earth"; and it was so. And the earth brought forth grass, the herb that yields seed according to its kind, and the tree that yields fruit, whose seed is in itself according to its kind. And God saw that it was good. So the evening and the morning were the third day.

Genesis 1:9-13

Then God said, "Let there be lights in the firmament of the heavens to divide the day from the night; and let them be for signs and seasons, and for days and years; and let them be for lights in the firmament of the heavens to give light on the earth"; and it was so. Then God made two great lights: the greater light to rule the day, and the lesser light to rule the night. He made the stars also. God set them in the firmament of the heavens to give light on the earth, and to rule over the day and over the night, and to divide the light from the darkness. And God saw that it was good. So the evening and the morning were the fourth day.

GENESIS 1:14-19

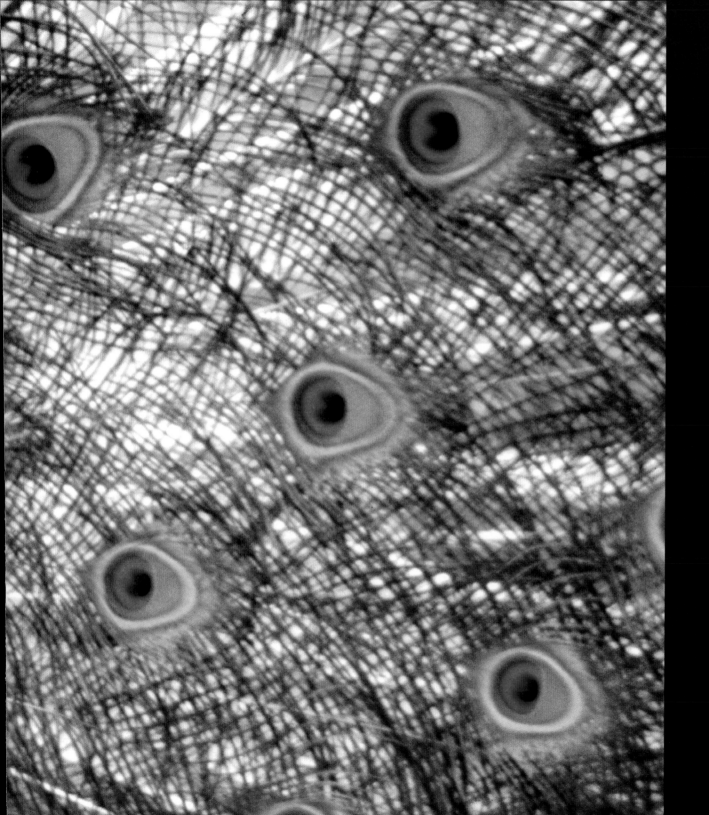

Then God said, "Let the waters abound with an abundance of living creatures, and let birds fly above the earth across the face of the firmament of the heavens." So God created great sea creatures and every living thing that moves, with which the waters abounded, according to their kind, and every winged bird according to its kind. And God saw that it was good. And God blessed them, saying, "Be fruitful and multiply, and fill the waters in the seas, and let birds multiply on the earth." So the evening and the morning were the fifth day.

GENESIS 1:20-23

6. Wildebeest, Ngorongoro Crater, Tanzania

Then God said, "Let the earth bring forth the living creature according to its kind: cattle and creeping thing and beast of the earth, each according to its kind"; and it was so. And God made the beast of the earth according to its kind, cattle according to its kind, and everything that creeps on the earth according to its kind. And God saw that it was good.

Then God said, "Let Us make man in Our image, according to Our likeness; let them have dominion over the fish of the sea, over the birds of the air, and over the cattle, over all the earth and over every creeping thing that creeps on the earth." So God created man in His own image; in the image of God He created him; male and female He created them.

GENESIS 1:24-27

7. Father and Son, Chitral, Pakistan

THE IMAGE OF GOD

The Glory of Man

RIC ERGENBRIGHT
Essays by Dana Ergenbright

Tyndale House Publishers, Inc., Wheaton, Illinois

Visit Tyndale's exciting Web site at www.tyndale.com

The Image of God: The Glory of Man
Copyright © 2004 by Ric Ergenbright. All rights reserved
All photographs © 2004 by Ric Ergenbright. All rights reserved.

Unless otherwise indicated, all Scripture quotations are taken from the *Holy Bible,* New King James Version.
Copyright © 1979, 1980, 1982, 1991 by Thomas Nelson, Inc. Used by permission. All rights reserved.

Scripture quotations marked NLT are taken from the *Holy Bible,* New Living Translation, copyright © 1996.
Used by permission of Tyndale House Publishers, Inc., Wheaton, Illinois 60189. All rights reserved.

Scripture quotations marked NIV are taken from the *Holy Bible,* New International Version®. NIV®.
Copyright © 1973, 1978, 1984 by International Bible Society. Used by permission of Zondervan Publishing House.
All rights reserved.

Scripture quotations marked NASB are taken from the *New American Standard Bible,* © 1960, 1962, 1963, 1968,
1971, 1972, 1973, 1975, 1977, 1995 by The Lockman Foundation. Used by permission.

Scripture quotations marked ESV are from *The Holy Bible,* English Standard Version, copyright © 2001
by Crossway Bibles, a division of Good News Publishers. Used by permission. All rights reserved.

Library of Congress Cataloging-in-Publication Data
Ergenbright, Ric.
    The Image of God : the glory of man / Ric and Dana Ergenbright.
        p. cm.
Includes bibliographical references.
    ISBN 0-8423-3984-1 (alk. paper)
    1. Man (Christian theology) I. Ergenbright, Dana. II. Title.
BT701.3.E74 2004
233— dc22

                    2003021189

Printed in China
09 08 07 06 05 04
6 5 4 3 2 1

8. Sunrise, Lake Dal, Kashmir

This book is dedicated to Dan and Sharon Dillard, whose love of God and passion for His glory define every facet of their lives, shining the light of Jesus upon all who know them.

TO THE READER

The photographs in this book represent selected moments from my travels over the past thirty years, particularly those moments involving people. Some of these encounters were brief, without a word being spoken; yet something was shared—a look, a smile, a gesture—that clearly spoke to our common humanity. We were alike, so we could communicate, and we were different, so we had something to share. It was in such moments of understanding that these pictures were made and in which they still speak today. Although a photograph is unalterably bound by the vision of the photographer and the unique moment in time that it records, the subject matter it conveys is often able to speak to people of all places and all generations. It is with this understanding that I set these pictures before you, knowing that the limited scope of my travels and the personal biases of my vision make it impossible for me to adequately illustrate the sweep of human history addressed in this book. My hope instead is that the subject matter itself will transcend the bounds of time and place to present a faithful view of the common nature and shared experience of all mankind. It is my prayer that this book will inspire you to look anew at the awesome reality of man's special calling, to faithfully live as the image of God on earth, for the good of all peoples and the glory and honor of our Creator.

ACKNOWLEDGMENTS

There is something special about Tyndale House Publishers; I saw it on my first visit there many years ago and still see it today. It is a love of God and a desire to share that love, which shows itself in an extraordinary friendliness that brings out the best in others. It has been a joy to work with Tyndale on this book, and I thank Ron Beers for that opportunity. I'd also like to express special thanks to Tammy Faxel for her steadfast support and encouragement, despite my frequent delays; to Dave Lindstedt for his exceptional editing and valuable contributions to the book's style and content; and to Travis Thrasher for always being there to smooth communication and teach us not to take ourselves too seriously.

9. *Happy Face, Hangzhou, China*

Contents

When I began my travel career, my passion was seeing and photographing the differences between the world's cultures. But time and experience have shown me that they are more alike than not. People everywhere laugh when they are happy, cry when they are hurt, and ask the same "big" questions about life. Who am I? Where did I come from? should I live? The all-encompassing question of the ages, however, was asked by David in Psalm 8: "What is man?"

How we answer this question determines the way we live, because our views of people, nature, and God are all founded on our perception of man. It defines our understanding and expression of love in our families

and establishes the deity or thing that we worship and serve.

This book considers man as he is portrayed in the Bible. Made in the glorious image of God, man rejected the design of his Creator and thus became a broken image. But God, in His compassion, provided healing and restoration so that man might once again live as God's glorious

What an exalted view of man! Here is the foundation for the abundant life that God intends for all mankind—a life characterized by love that gives, rule that serves, and worship that trusts and obeys God. Restored to the image of God in which he was created, man is truly glorious. This book celebrates that glory.

INTRODUCTION

Journeys, great and small, often take us where we least expect. Seventeen years ago I could not have imagined I would someday write a book about the perfection of God and the glory of man. Back then, I didn't believe God existed, and I didn't see man as glorious. I had chosen to walk a different path, and God was not on it. But shielding my eyes and denying God's truth didn't make it untrue; it simply blinded me to reality. A day was to come when God would graciously open my eyes to see that He had not only been on "my" path, He had directed my every step to bring me to exactly the right place at just the right time to meet Him.

The introduction to *The Art of God* told of my journey from unbelief and rebellion against God to faith and surrender to His rule over my life. How far He took me from worshiping the creation to worshiping its Creator— how great was my sin, yet how much greater His forgiveness! What joy He gave me, and what splendor He showed me, as He lovingly and patiently opened my eyes to see His glory in the world He had made and the Word He had spoken in the Bible.

Yet my journey was only beginning. As I prepared to write this book, I realized I was still blind to God's greatest creation of all. Focusing on God's revelation in nature, I had thoroughly ignored what His Word reveals about man, who was made in His very image. This wasn't a simple oversight; it was the direct outworking of my true affections. Seeing God's glory in nature was easy, for I'd always loved nature. But seeing God's glory in man was unthinkable, because I didn't like man. In fact, I hated him for his evil ways. This inconsistency arose from a synthesis of my new and old views of reality. My outlook on nature was now that of the Bible, but my outlook on man was that of the daily news. Until I saw man as God saw man, I could never write this book. Thus a new leg of my journey began, as God once again used His razor-sharp Word to operate on the eyes of my heart, enabling me to see the glory of man as revealed in the Bible.

When I wrote *The Art of God*, I used Psalm 8:3-4 to extol the glory of the heavens: "When I consider Your heavens, the work of Your fingers, the moon and the stars, which You have ordained, what is man that You are mindful of him, and the son of man that You visit him?" I mistakenly thought David was contrasting the perfection of nature against the unworthiness of man. When I read on, however, I saw that he was actually marveling at the extreme worth of man and the exalted position God had given him: "For You have made him a little lower than the angels, and You have crowned him with glory and honor. You have made him to have

11. Camel Caravan, Dunhuang, China

dominion over the works of Your hands; You have put all things under his feet" (Psalm 8:5-6). Man was the only creature made in God's image, made to imitate His love and His rule, and made to worship Him. Reflecting God's glory more than any other created thing, man was truly glorious.

However, man was not content to reflect God's glory, and in trying to establish his own glory, he lost it entirely. Made to love God and others, he was now isolated and alone, filled with bitterness and strife. Made to humbly serve God and rule the creation, he was now proud and self-serving. Made to glory in God, he now gloried in himself and in false gods. But God did not cast him off. He promised to send a Redeemer who would rescue man from his darkness and restore him to his original glory. At God's appointed place and time, God the Son, the true Image of God (being coequal and coeternal with the Father), came into the world in the form of a man named Jesus (Colossians 1:12-23). In Him all the glory of God shone forth, and those who turned from their own darkness to His light began to reflect His glory. Keeping their eyes upon Jesus, they were increasingly restored to His image.

How glorious, then, is man! The glory of nature pales in comparison. For God the Son came to earth for the sake of man, not for mountains, forests, or seas. And because He loved me while I was in darkness, I should love all men. But I don't. The more I look to Jesus, the more I see the darkness of my own heart—the pride, selfishness, and lack of love—making me more aware of my need for His transforming light. This humbling process is the very means by which God moves us toward our destination of being "conformed to the image of His Son" (Romans 8:29).

I thank God for granting faith to my daughter Dana and uniting her path with mine to produce *The Image of God*. Looking back, it is easy to see God's providence in our lives that prepared us for this effort. From her earliest years, Dana loved to organize and to learn, but who could imagine that this child, who grouped animal crackers and read encyclopedias for fun, would someday write this book? Yet that was God's itinerary for her. The breadth of this book's subject demanded the organizational skills Dana

You saw me before I was born. Every day of my life was recorded in your book. Every moment was laid out before a single day had passed. PSALM 139:16 NLT

was born with and added to as a history major in college—the ability to do extensive research and condense voluminous information into a usable form. The complexity of the subject required the skills Dana has gained as a teacher—the talent to simplify complicated information and convey it in a clear and engaging manner.

The visual nature of the book called for images and experiences from my lifelong work in the field of photographic travel. Beginning at the age of eight, when my father founded America's first tour company for "camera fans," my life was filled with pictures and stories of far-off lands and exotic cultures that stirred my imagination and took me on great flights of fantasy to the ends of the earth. In time, those journeys became real, and the pictures and stories were of my own adventures in some of the world's most beautiful and remote locations. I shot nearly a quarter of a million photographs in the first two decades of my travels, and not one was intended to glorify God. But the designs of a sovereign Creator are not bound by the purposes of created things. As the psalmist says

12. Sisters, Suzhou, China   13. Merchant, Tashkurghan, Afghanistan

in Psalm 139:16 (NLT), "You saw me before I was born. Every day of my life was recorded in your book. Every moment was laid out before a single day had passed." Despite my intentions when I took the photographs, every picture in this book was directed by God for the purpose of His glory.

The Image of God is unique in its concept and design. Combining the historical narrative of man's creation, fall, and redemption, with photographs of real people in real places, it presents this vitally important topic in the language of everyday life, not the abstract philosophical terminology of the classroom. This is a true story about real people and the true and living God, not an intangible idea that is disconnected from daily experience. From the beginning, God has communicated His truth to man through images and stories of real-life events. Following His example, using current-day pictures of the worldwide family of man, we have endeavored to illustrate the eternal relevance and life-changing power of this story, which is for all people of all nations.

Our journey in creating this book has now come to an end, and your journey in reading it has just begun. May God grant you eyes to see His glory in the faces on these pages, faces illuminated by the light of His Word.

14. Father and Son, Ambato, Ecuador   15. Rajasthani Girl, Jaisalmer, Rajasthan, India

16. *Girl with Grandmother, Calbuco, Chile*

Made to Love

What a gift it is to be unique. Of the billions of people on earth, of the billions who have lived before, no one else shares your exact combination of characteristics. The shape of your nose, the pattern of your fingerprints, the sound of your voice, the colors and tastes you like, the things that make you smile or cry—you are a masterpiece so complex that you cannot even fully understand yourself. Every other person is just as unique, just as complex, just as much a masterpiece.

Who could have designed this glorious rainbow of humanity, this infinite variety? Only God, the Creator of the world and everything in it, who gives life and breath to all creatures, the depth of whose wisdom and knowledge no one can grasp, and whose ways are unsearchable. It is He who created the first man and woman, from whom He made every nation on the face of the earth.

Why has God done this? Because God's nature is love, and love delights in giving. God the Father, God the Son, and God the Holy Spirit have eternally loved one another. And because love and communication are at the core of God's being, we who are stamped with His glorious image are made for relationships of love and communication—with Him and with others.

But what is love? Love is action, a sacrificial giving of oneself to another, often in spite of emotions. Love does not live for itself or look inward; instead, it is oriented toward others and their needs. Love perseveres despite changing circumstances and changing emotions. No relationship can endure or grow without it. God's love enables us to properly love ourselves and others.

MAN

God created man in His own image;
in the image of God He created him.

GENESIS 1:27

God formed the first man, Adam, from the dust of the ground. He breathed the breath of life into his nostrils, and man became a living being. Everything in the newly created world revealed aspects of its Creator, but nothing revealed Him as fully as man. God chose to make mankind in His own image and likeness—not just a little higher than the monkeys, but a little lower than God Himself. No other creature was so exalted.

How glorious was man! Like God, he could think, speak, work, rest, and enjoy the creation. Like God, he could organize, develop, and beautify the world. Only man, of all God's creatures, was given these God-like abilities. But he was not God. Unlike God, he could not create something from nothing, nor could he ever attain the infinite wisdom, strength, and glory of his Creator. Yet, bearing the image of God, he was the crown of creation, the glorious reflection of God on earth.

The source of man's glory, however, was not his abilities—it was his relationship of love and communication with God. Adam walked and talked face-to-face with the Almighty Maker of heaven and earth, who was not only God, He was Adam's God. In this person-to-person relationship, this covenant established by God, Adam was designed to grow in godliness to reflect God's glory ever more brightly. Man was glorious because God was glorious, and man revealed God's glory to the world.

Just as God's hands formed the first man from the dust of the earth, His hands formed you and me in our mothers' wombs. Before the foundation of the world, each of us was a thought in God's mind, purposefully created with a unique combination of characteristics and talents. Not only that, He also talks to us, and we can talk to Him. He knows us, and we can know Him. Though God is high and exalted above His creation, you and I can have a personal relationship with Him. Our sense of worth comes not by looking at ourselves but by looking at the God who made us in His image.

31

17. Prince Zia, Chitral, Pakistan

The LORD God formed man of the dust of the ground, and breathed into his nostrils the breath of life; and man became a living being. GENESIS 2:7

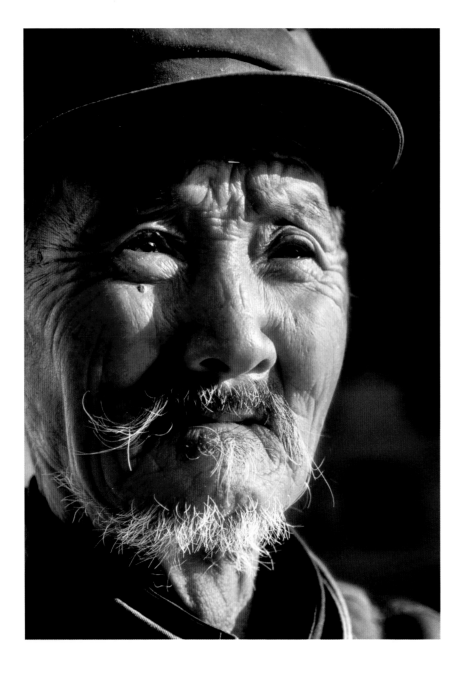

The Pathan tribesmen of Pakistan's Northwest Frontier Province are famous for their gun-making and fighting skills, both of which were used against the British during the years of British imperial rule on the Indian subcontinent. Assuming I was British and attempting to provoke a fight, this tribesman glared at me and said, "My grandfather killed your grandfather, and my father killed your father." The implication was perfectly clear: I represented the next generation in his equation. Then Mahmud, my guide and interpreter, saved the day by saying, "Then you must be friends, because this man is an American, and his grandfathers fought the British too!" ➲

18. Vendor, Dunhuang, China 19. Farmer, Bamiyan Valley, Afghanistan 20. Gun Maker, Kohat Pass, Pakistan

The Spirit of God has made me, and the breath of the Almighty gives me life. JOB 33:4

❝ One of the strangest encounters of my career was with this Kashmiri man in the village bazaar at Pahalgam. Even though I photographed him for at least ten minutes, he never blinked or changed expression once. He was so completely calm and his stare was so thoroughly intense, I felt our roles had been reversed. The camera may have been in my hands, but it was he who saw the subject more clearly.

21. Merchant, Pahalgam, Kashmir, India 22. Olive Farmer, Portugal 23. Altiplano Native, Cuzco, Peru

Know that the LORD, He is God; it is He who has made us, and not we ourselves. PSALM 100:3

 Headwear is one of the world's great cultural distinctives. The brightly colored turbans worn by the men of Rajasthan, India, are made with more than fifteen yards of fabric and are an effective barrier against the heat of the Thar Desert.

The red earthen-dyed hair of a young Masai warrior, or *moran,* is sometimes braided with a lion's tail, a badge of bravery indicating he killed the lion with his spear. Once a quest of all *morani,* this practice is now forbidden by the governments of Kenya and Tanzania. ↩↩

24. Camel Herder, Pushkar, India 25. Tyrolean Man, Hallstatt, Austria 26. Masai Warrior, Kenya

The Lord God said, "It is not good that man should be alone; I will make a helper comparable to him."

Man was glorious, but he was incomplete. To show Adam what he lacked, God brought all the animals to him to study and name. When Adam finished his task, he realized there was no other creature like him. He was the only human being on earth. He was alone.

It was not good for Adam to be alone because God, whose image he bore, was not alone. From all eternity, God was one God but three distinct persons—Father, Son, and Holy Spirit—each equally God, existing in a personal relationship of love and communication. These three persons made man in their image: "Let Us make man in Our image, according to Our likeness" (Genesis 1:26, NASB). Inherent in man's nature, then, is the need for a personal relationship with an equal. Adam could not properly reflect the image of God without a companion. So God caused the man to fall asleep, took a rib from his side, and fashioned it into the first woman, Eve. She was a perfect companion for Adam, equal in every way—equally made in the image of God, equally blessed and commissioned by God.

Although God made man and woman entirely equal, He also made them fundamentally different, each reflecting different aspects of His character. God made man to lead, provide, and protect; He made woman to nurture, help, and support. Because each one needs the strengths of the other, giving is necessary. Man is not independent of woman, nor is woman independent of man (1 Corinthians 11:11). Only *together* do they exemplify God's rich nature. Because man and woman are equal *and* different, they complete each other.

27. *Woman in Kimono, Miyajima, Japan*

The LORD *God fashioned into a woman the rib which He had taken from the man, and brought her to the man.* GENESIS 2:22 NASB

The *tika,* commonly seen on the forehead of Hindu women, is worn to signify they are married. It is also believed to be a source of life and energy, symbolizing concentration, intuition, and knowledge. ↩↩

28. Ladakhi Woman, Leh, Ladakh, India 29. Folk Dancer, Segovia, Spain 30. Rajasthani Bride, Udaipur, Rajasthan, India

Adam said: "This at last is bone of my bones and flesh of my flesh."

GENESIS 2:23 ESV

43

↻ *Uygurs* (pronounced *we-gurs*) are the predominant ethnic population in western China. They are a Turkic people descended from the Huns, who came from central Asia, and have played a major role in the history of China and much of Asia. Their appearance is strikingly Western, contrasting sharply with the look of the Han Chinese, who are predominant in the rest of the country.

The delightful, smile-worn face of this fishwife from Japan's Izu Peninsula could well have been the model for the "happy face" icon that is used around the world to communicate joy. ➲

31. Uygur Woman, Turfan, China 32. Fishwife, Izu, Japan

Woman is the glory of man.

1 CORINTHIANS 11:7

45

☾ The colorful beadwork necklaces of the Masai women in Kenya and Tanzania present a strong contrast to the largely monochromatic landscape.

An even greater contrast is seen in the costumes of Ladakhi women, whose homeland, known as "Little Tibet," is in the high and barren foothills of the Himalayas. Here, even the most elaborate turquoise, coral, and silver jewelry is overshadowed by a unique traditional headdress, called a *perak,* that is said to have been designed by a long-ago queen who was self-conscious about the size of her ears. Sporting two large woolen ear flaps and a turquoise-studded hood that runs down the back, the *perak* is not only protective, but the quantity and quality of its stones also make it a status symbol. **☞**

33. Masai Woman, Kenya 34. Ladakhi Dancer, Leh, Ladakh, India

Marriage

A man shall leave his father and mother and be joined to his wife, and they shall become one flesh. GENESIS 2:24

As equal yet distinct persons, Adam and Eve reflected the relational aspects of God's triune nature. And because Eve's body was formed from Adam's rib, they also mirrored God's oneness. They were literally of one flesh, and Adam's name for Eve reflected this: "She shall be called Woman *[Ishah]*, because she was taken out of Man *[Ish]*" (Genesis 2:23, NASB). As the Father, Son, and Spirit are one, so are man and woman to be one.

The relationship God established between Adam and Eve is the pattern for the covenant relationship of marriage, wherein a man and a woman unite with each other and become one flesh. Looking to God's love as his model, a man is to love and cherish his bride, to care for her as he cares for his own body. A woman is to respect her husband and submit to his leadership in the same way that she honors God and submits to Him. What a blessing God has bestowed on men and women through this lifelong relationship of self-sacrificing love. As we faithfully honor our marriage vows, we are no longer slaves to our fickle emotions. We are truly free to love.

Our essential nature as men and women is most completely expressed as husbands and wives. Mirroring the relationship between God and His people, a husband steadfastly loves his wife, and a wife thankfully receives and responds to his love (Ephesians 5:22-33). Because a man needs a helper to attain his full purpose, and a woman best expresses her nature through helping (Genesis 2:18, 20-22), it is in the marriage relationship that their individual strengths are most fully realized. This cooperative, life-giving union becomes the shelter under which succeeding generations are nurtured; it becomes the source of all other social relationships—parent and child, brother and sister, neighbor and neighbor.

35. Newlyweds, Rajasthan, India

Husbands should love their wives as their own bodies. He who loves his wife loves himself.
Ephesians 5:28 ESV

What a gift from God it is to be able to capture a moment in time on film, to remember a day when we were young and strong. "For, 'All men are like grass, and all their glory is like the flowers of the field; the grass withers and the flowers fall, but the word of the Lord stands forever'" (1 Peter 1:24-25, NIV).

36. Forever Young, Linz, Austria 37. Husband and Wife, Bamiyan, Afghanistan 38. Ric and Jill Ergenbright by Scott Loring

The covenantal nature of marriage, ordained by God in the second chapter of Genesis, is the foundation of all wedding ceremonies, regardless of culture or religion. In most societies, rings are exchanged as symbols of the binding, everlasting reality of this covenant. In Hindu weddings such as this one in a small village of western India, a knotted cord—or in this case, two shawls—is also used to emphasize the sacred union of the bride and groom. Hence, they have "tied the knot." ➲

What God has joined together,
let not man separate.

MATTHEW 19:6

39. Wedding, Kamakura, Japan 40. Hindu Wedding, Rajasthan, India 41. Wedding Knot, Rajasthan, India

50

CHILDREN

God blessed them, and God said to them,
*   "Be fruitful and multiply."* GENESIS 1:28

God gave Adam and Eve a remarkable wedding gift: the ability to have children. As they portrayed God's unity by becoming one flesh, they would further reflect His image by bearing children in their own image and likeness. Through God's blessing on their loving union, Adam and Eve would begin their God-given task of multiplying and filling the earth. Their children would bear their image physically, showing characteristics of both father and mother. Their children would also emulate their parents spiritually, enjoying a personal relationship of love and communication with God. From the womb, they would be His children, and He would be their God.

Through the outworking of the parent–child relationship, God intended that the nature of heaven would be more fully revealed on earth. As Adam and Eve learned how to be parents by looking to the love of God the Father, they would tenderly, patiently, and sacrificially provide for their children's needs. Through their example and through loving discipline and communication, they would teach their children to glorify God. Out of gratitude, their children would honor and obey them, imitating God the Son. All family members would gain a deeper understanding of their identity as children of God and a greater love for their heavenly Father. By the power of God the Spirit, Adam and Eve's home would reflect the love of God's heavenly home.

53

42. Friends, Kashgar, China

*Behold, children are a gift
of the LORD.* Psalm 127:3 NASB

When I returned to the Himalayan region of Ladakh one year after taking this picture, I brought a print to give to the girl's family. To find them, I showed the picture to some people at the local bazaar, and a young boy grabbed it and signaled me to follow him. Winding down a maze of narrow alleys and ducking through numerous head-threatening doorways, we eventually emerged in a small interior courtyard that was flanked by several doors. After disappearing behind one of the doors, the boy quickly returned with the girl and a large crowd of excited family members, who were rejoicing as if I'd come to award a million-dollar sweepstakes prize. Food and drink soon appeared, and a hearty celebration began, uniting us—from worlds apart—in a shared moment of joy and common understanding. ➲

43. Erin, California 44. Apple Vendor, Ladakh, India 45. Sister and Little Brother, Kathmandu, Nepal

Children's children are the crown of old men,
and the glory of children is their father.

PROVERBS 17:6

Everywhere I've traveled, nothing has so effectively opened the door to communication and understanding as expressing an appreciation of someone's child. The face of even the hardest man softens with pride when his son or daughter is being photographed. For a brief and wonderful moment, our defenses come down as together we focus on the child, sharing a common emotion that connects us as human beings.

46. Girl with Grandfather, Peshawar, Pakistan 47. Father and Son, Chitral, Pakistan, 48. Safety Zone, Ecuador

The mercy of the LORD is from everlasting to everlasting on those who fear Him, and His righteousness to children's children, to such as keep His covenant, and to those who remember His commandments to do them.
PSALM 103:17-18

59

☾ There are magical moments when we glimpse a fleeting expression that is so compelling our minds seem to freeze it in time. These visions rarely occur when we have a camera in hand, and if they do, the camera is almost never focused in the right place. Many such moments are recorded in my mind, but few are on film. This is one of the exceptions, taken in Kashmir, India, as a young girl glanced my way at just the right instant.

49. Kashmiri Girl, Srinagar, India 50. Festival Dress, Takamatsu, Japan 51. Young Hiker, Kitzbühel, Austria

You formed my inward parts; You covered me in my mother's womb. I will praise You, for I am fearfully and wonderfully made; marvelous are Your works, and that my soul knows very well. My frame was not hidden from You, when I was made in secret, and skillfully wrought in the lowest parts of the earth. Your eyes saw my substance, being yet unformed. And in Your book they all were written, the days fashioned for me, when as yet there were none of them.

Psalm 139:13-16

52. All in the Family, Connemara, Ireland

God said to them, "…fill the earth." GENESIS 1:28

As image bearers of God, all people have great worth. The clearest way to show one's love for God, who cannot be seen, is to love one's neighbors, who reflect His image. In fact, only those who love their neighbors can truly be said to love God (1 John 4:7-8).

God's infinite personality is displayed in the diversity of temperaments and talents found in the human community. Whether naturally reserved or exuberant, cautious or bold; whether drawn to details or concepts, to animals or children; whether gifted with paintbrush or hammer, with words or numbers, every person mirrors traits of God, enabling others to appreciate and love God more. As people use their gifts to bless each other, filling up what others lack, these differences are a radiant reflection of God's rich character as well as of His love.

Because we all manifest God in unique ways, we need to be in relationships with other people in order to fully appreciate and love God. We were designed to glorify God and to live not only for ourselves but also for our neighbors. We are sons and daughters of Adam and Eve and sons and daughters of God, who has knit us together into the family of man. We were designed to shine forth the glorious love of God to the ends of the earth by pouring ourselves out for our spouses, children, and neighbors.

63

53. Friends, Otavalo, Ecuador

He made from one
man every nation of
mankind to live on all
the face of the earth,
having determined
their appointed times
and the boundaries of
their habitation.

ACTS 17:26 NASB

54. *Pushkar Camel Fair, Rajasthan, India* 55. *Portovenere, Italy* 56. *Taking Charge, Darjeeling, India*

Sing to the LORD a new song,
and His praise from the ends
of the earth. ISAIAH 42:10

↻ Perched on a cliff overlooking the Mediterranean, Manarola is one of five villages that make up the renowned Cinque Terra on Italy's Ligurian Coast. Linked by train and trail through steeply terraced hills and vineyards, each village is about two miles from its neighbor. In 2001, the entire eleven-mile stretch became an Italian national park.

Dominating the fabled Himalayan Valley of Hunza yet dwarfed beneath the giant peaks of the Karakoram Range, the village of Baltit (Karimabad) has long been heralded as one of the world's most remote and idyllic spots. Thought to be the inspiration and model for Shangri-la in James Hilton's novel *Lost Horizon*, Hunza is renowned for the purity and healthiness of its environment and lifestyle, which has produced an extraordinary number of active centenarians. In years past, under the rule of a benevolent king, or *mir*, the ultimate penalty for the worst crime in Hunza was banishment from the kingdom. Today, however, many young people, attracted by the material goods introduced by tourists, have voluntarily left the valley for the promised "riches" of the outside world. ↻

57. Manarola, Cinque Terra, Italy 58. Karimabad, Hunza, Pakistan

The LORD *looks from heaven; He sees all the sons of men.... He fashions their hearts individually; He considers all their works.* PSALM 33:13, 15

What is the proper perspective? Is there another way to look at a subject that will reveal more information and provide greater understanding? These are vital questions that we should ask ourselves, whether in the concrete world or the visual world or in the abstract realm of ideas. Humans commonly see the world straight on, from about three to seven feet above the ground. A mouse sees it from the ground looking up, and a bird sees it from the sky looking down. Each sees reality, but every viewpoint and interpretation is different. So which view is the proper one? None of them. Only God sees and knows all things, and He has revealed all truth to the world through His creation, His spoken word in the Bible, and especially through the person of His Son, Jesus Christ. If we study all of these means from every possible angle, He will grant us the proper perspective we seek. And that view will always reveal His glory.

59. Overview, Brugge, Belgium 60. Rush Hour, Beijing, China 61. Champs d'Elysees, Paris, France

Made to Rule

Each person is wonderfully different, yet we are remarkably the same. From north to south and east to west, we act in surprisingly similar ways. From 2004 B.C. to A.D. 2004, human behavior has been amazingly consistent. The moment we open our eyes as infants, we begin studying our world. As we grow in our understanding of how the world *is,* we begin dreaming about how it *could be* and then work to unleash its potential. Under human hands, a desert becomes a fertile field, a piece of marble becomes an intricately carved masterpiece, a handful of sand becomes a glass window, a tree becomes a magnificent ship. We are perpetually working with the earth's elements—and transforming the world in the process.

What impels us? Of all earth's creatures, why do we alone do purposeful and creative work? Because God works, and we were made in His image. Had He chosen, He could have created the world in all its fullness in a split second. Instead, He crafted His creation over the course of six days, developing it and making it more glorious each day, pouring into it life, breath, wisdom, and beauty. Apart from His continuing care, nothing could exist—even now, our every breath is dependent upon Him. He needs nothing from us, and we need everything from Him. Though He is the sovereign King of creation, He is not ashamed to serve us. This King rules by serving.

Astonishingly, God entrusted His kingdom to two of His creatures—a man and a woman. As king and queen, they were to rule over all the earth—the plants and trees, the fish of the sea, the birds of the sky, the cattle and everything that creeps on the earth. The man and woman began their rule in a garden, which they were to develop and cultivate (literally, to *serve*). Following God's example, they were to exercise their dominion by making the world increasingly glorious each day—working, beautifying, and enjoying it. Through their service, the earth would reflect the glory of heaven. True kings are servant kings.

LEARNING

*Since the creation of the world God's invisible qualities—
his eternal power and divine nature—have been clearly
seen, being understood from what has been made.*

ROMANS 1:20 NIV

In order to rule over God's creation, Adam had to learn about it. By studying what God had made, Adam would grow in his understanding of the world, himself, and God, who was marvelously revealed in all He had made. Adam would rule not as a detached dictator but as a close benefactor, intimately acquainted with his subjects.

Adam's first lesson involved naming all the animals over which he was to rule. They were to be his helpers—pulling his plow, providing eggs and cheese for his table and wool for his blankets. The bees would teach him about cooperation, the otters about delighting in work, the lions about courage, and the ants about diligence. Adam would also learn that just as each of these creatures had a mate, he too needed a companion. So God fashioned a woman to be with Adam. Together they would study and tend God's creation and glorify Him by enjoying His excellent works.

Because God is revealed in all things, learning would be a thrilling task. God's wisdom, creativity, power, and love shone everywhere—in the orderly, immense heavens, the intricacy and variety of the flowers, and the continual provision of food and water. And this was just the beginning! The universe was full of secrets and mysteries waiting to be unraveled, from the magnetic field to the structure of the atom. There were things that Adam and Eve and their descendants would never fully understand because they were only creatures. How could their limited minds encompass the Creator's mind? God knew all things, whereas they knew only what He revealed to them. But there was still so much they *could* know, and every bit of knowledge they gained would deepen their love for God and their understanding of the way He rules His creation. Thus, their learning would prepare them to rule like He rules.

63. At the Beach, Santa Monica, California

Great are the works of the LORD; *they are studied by all who delight in them.*

PSALM 111:2 NASB

🎧 Learning is frequently a shared experience in which both teacher and pupil gain understanding and enjoyment. Many national park visitors have learned that golden mantle ground squirrels will eagerly take food from human hands—and the squirrels have learned that wherever vacationers gather there is food to be had.

64. Pals, Lake Louise, Alberta, Canada 65. Homework, Saidu Sharif, Swat, Pakistan 66. Water Works Park, Seattle, Washington

67. Co-op Classroom, Harbin, China 68. Professor, Beijing, China 69. Dana and Boh, Southern California

Can you search out the deep things of God?
Can you find out the limits of the Almighty?

JOB 11:7

As humans, we continually seek to learn about the world and ourselves—from our earliest lessons in problem solving, through our childhood years in the classroom, to more intricate investigations of mathematical formulas and complex scientific theories. Because all truth is from God, and He is unable to lie or contradict Himself (Titus 1:2; 1 John 1:5), we can truly grow in wisdom and knowledge by diligently weighing our observations against God's perfect revelation in nature and the Bible. Because truth is truth, there is no middle ground; all contradictions demand resolution. God makes no mistakes, so if His world does not appear to agree with His Word, we must go back to the drawing board to reconsider the facts or review our biblical interpretation.

LABOR

Let them rule over the fish of the sea and over the birds of the sky and over the cattle and over all the earth, and over every creeping thing that creeps on the earth.

GENESIS 1:26 NASB

With the knowledge Adam and Eve gained through their study of God's creation, they would begin the task of tending the world, according to God's model. Over the course of six days, God worked with the raw materials He had made, restructuring and developing them. Light was separated from dark, the waters above the heavens from the waters below, the dry land from the sea. Separating and breaking down His works, God made the creation reveal His glories more each day.

This was the same type of restructuring work that Adam and Eve were to do. There was soil to till and farm, grain to harvest and grind into flour, fibers to be woven into cloth, dyes to extract from plants, deeply buried ores to mine and refine into precious metals, trees to cut and mill, flocks to tend, and rivers, seas, and distant lands to explore. What an honor and a responsibility it would be to take the work of God's hands into their own hands!

As God's representatives, Adam and Eve were to develop and care for the world the way God did, bringing forth its potential. This would entail caring for it, not destroying or squandering it. Though their work would be hard, it would be deeply satisfying because they were workers by nature. God is a worker; as His image bearers, Adam and Eve would also find great joy in working for God's glory.

79

70. Working the Well, Rajasthan, India

*Six days you shall labor
and do all your work.*

DEUTERONOMY 5:13

Traveling in the Himalayan foothills of the
Vale of Kashmir, it is common to share the road
with herds of goats, which are raised for their
world-famous *pashmina* (or cashmere) wool.
Aware of the long shadows cast by the early
morning light, I scrambled up the road bank to
capture this "shadow picture" of the goats and
their herder as they passed by. ➲

71. Fishermen, Nazaré, Portugal 72. Goatherd, Kashmir, India 73. Winnowing Grain, Bamiyan, Afghanistan

Whatever you do,
do your work heartily,
as for the Lord rather
than for men.
Colossians 3:23 NASB

🎧 Farming in India and most of southwestern Asia is rarely mechanized. It is common to see workers winnowing grain by hand, but it never fails to excite my photographic senses. Often, however, the surrounding environment is so cluttered that it is difficult to get a decent picture of this colorful activity. My answer to this dilemma was to find a different point of view that would simplify the background and thereby strengthen the visual story. In this scene, the easiest way to achieve a clean perspective was to get down on the ground and shoot upward, using the sky as a seamless backdrop. An added benefit of using this technique is that it usually evokes a smile, if not an incredulous laugh, from the subject.

74. Plowing, Swat Valley, Pakistan 75. Huaso and Sheep, Centinela, Chile 76. Winnowing, near Jodhpur, India

An excellent wife who can find?...She rises while it is yet night and provides food for her household and portions for her maidens. She considers a field and buys it; with the fruit of her hands she plants a vineyard....She looks well to the ways of her household and does not eat the bread of idleness....Give her of the fruit of her hands, and let her works praise her in the gates.

PROVERBS 31:10, 15-16, 27, 31 ESV

At 550 feet below sea level, the Turfan Depression in China's Xinjiang region is the second-lowest spot on earth. Extremely hot in summer, it is irrigated by a series of ancient, underground channels that carry water from the snowcapped Tian Shan range some fifty miles to the north. The result is a desert oasis that is perfectly suited to the cultivation of grapes, which hang luxuriously from arbors throughout the area. Here a young woman cuts a large clump of grapes for the enjoyment of her guests.

77. Wash Day, Udaipur, Rajasthan, India 78. Picking Grapes, Turfan, China 79. Sweeping, Jaisalmer, Rajasthan, India

ART & ARCHITECTURE

Out of the ground the LORD *God made every tree grow that is pleasant to the sight.* GENESIS 2:9

As the supreme artist, God filled the world with masterpieces that reflect His beauty and glory—fiery gemstones, delicate flowers, spectacular panoramas, and stirring melodies. The universe itself is an architectural wonder, with its solid foundation, mighty mountain pillars, and vaulted ceiling, attesting to the wisdom and immovability of its Builder.

Of all God's earthly creatures, only Adam and Eve and their descendants had the ability to appreciate the art and architecture of God. With God's beauty and wisdom as their standard and God's Spirit as their guide, they too would create art. Through music, metalwork, carving, engraving, painting, weaving, dancing, drama, and literature, they would reflect the beauty they saw in God and His creation. They would also imitate God as they built houses and bridges and constructed works that were firm and lasting.

Future generations would build on their legacy, creating more skilled and beautiful art, constructing new and better buildings. As artists and builders copied the true Artist and Builder, the earth would increasingly mirror the glory and permanence of heaven, and mankind would increasingly reflect the beauty and wisdom of God.

80. Painter, Rumtek Monastery, Sikkim, India

Let them praise His name with the dance; let them sing praises to Him with the timbrel and harp.

Psalm 149:3

℃ A fascinating thing I have observed in my travels is that there is often a direct correlation between a culture's landscape and the vibrancy of its art. When the environment is lush and green with pronounced displays of seasonal color, the artwork of that region will generally be subdued. However, when the landscape is barren or monochromatic, the artwork will generally be exceptionally bright, with a preponderance of primary colors. The colorful textiles and turquoise jewelry of the Navajo people in the desert environment of the southwestern United States are examples of this common artistic response to one's surroundings.

81. Navajo Jewelry, Canyon de Chelly, Arizona 82. Harpist, Cuzco, Peru 83. Peking Opera, Beijing, China 84. Flutist, Thimphu Monastery, Bhutan

90

Every house is built by someone, but He who built all things is God.

HEBREWS 3:4

Shooting photos for an article for National Geographic's Traveler magazine, I was determined to reach a hard-to-find and harder-to-get-to viewpoint that overlooked Bavaria's famous Neuschwanstein Castle. Scouting for two days, I was frustrated again and again as every promising trail led me to a dead end. Then on the third morning, I was sure I'd found the correct route, but it required me to strap my camera bag and tripod onto my back and free climb up the face of a very steep cliff. As I reached the top and pulled myself over the edge, a startled and wide-eyed German photographer exclaimed, "Where in the world did you come from?" After we shot together for a couple of hours, he led me down a simple and well-worn path to the base of the mountain. ➲

85. Amber Palace, near Jaipur, India 86. Neuschwanstein Castle, Bavaria, Germany

A thousand years in Your sight
are like yesterday when it is past.

PSALM 90:4

↻ The two-thousand-year-old Pont du Gard was built by the Romans to enable the aqueduct from Uzes to Nimes to cross the canyon of the Pont River in what is today southern France. At 160 feet above the ground, it is the highest bridge the Romans ever built.

Another first-century Roman marvel is the 92-foot-high, 2,665-foot-long aqueduct in Segovia, Spain, which was built with twenty thousand interlocking granite blocks and no mortar. ➲

Begun in 220 B.C., the Great Wall extends more than four thousand miles across the mountains of northern China. ↻

87. Pont du Gard, Provence, France 88. Great Wall, China 89. Roman Aqueduct, Segovia, Spain

God saw everything that He had made,
and indeed it was very good. GENESIS 1:31

God evaluated His works after each day of Creation. As He surveyed the light; the land and sea; the grasses and trees; the sun, moon, and stars; the fish and the birds and the beasts of the earth, He declared them all good. But the fact that man was alone was not good because it did not properly reveal the relational nature of God—that of love and communication between equals. So He made woman and presented her to the man, and then He declared His creation very good.

Adam and Eve would evaluate their work in the same way, asking, "Is it good?" Then they would continue to work until it was *very* good; that is, until it revealed and glorified God. This did not mean that every task had to be magnificent—even housecleaning could glorify God by reflecting the way He maintained the creation. Most important was the attitude behind their work. The creation belonged to God, not to Adam and Eve, and as they recognized this and gave Him thanks for the privilege of being His stewards, their works would be acceptable to Him.

As communities developed, people would begin trading the works of their hands, reflecting the fairness and honesty of God by honest evaluations, fair prices, and just weights. The master-servant relationship between God and humanity would be mirrored in master-servant relationships that would develop within the community, with masters imitating their fair, kind Master in heaven, and servants working diligently and obediently, knowing they were actually serving God. Honesty and thankfulness in all these areas would glorify God, and both God and man would declare it very good.

90. Spices, Forcalquier, France

Dishonest scales are an abomination to the LORD, *but a just weight is His delight.*

PROVERBS II:I

☾ The fresh cucumbers, melons, and yogurt of northern Afghanistan will always hold a special place in my travel memories. When I arrived in the town of Tashkurghan, where this vegetable stall was located, I was so ill that I could barely stand up. But after a few days of eating these foods almost exclusively, I was revived and once again was able to appreciate the places and faces I'd come so far to see and photograph.

91. Vegetable Stall, Tashkurghan, Afghanistan 92. Produce Seller, Jodhpur, India

93. *Grape Vendor, Peshawar, Pakistan* 94. *Frying Potatoes, Ibarra, Ecuador* 95. *Making Bagels, Turfan, China* 96. *Vegetable Seller, Jaisalmer, Rajasthan, India*

If you sell anything to your neighbor or buy from your neighbor's hand, you shall not oppress one another.

LEVITICUS 25:14

Because the majority of people around the globe do not own a refrigerator, it is necessary for them to shop for fresh food every day. The markets they go to are usually outdoors and are typically made up of colorful stands or stalls where local vendors sell what they grow, make, or raise. But more than a place to buy food, the market is the customary gathering place of the community—where friends meet, news is shared, and gossip is exchanged. In short, it is the heart of the neighborhood, where something of interest is always to be found and smiles are easy to come by. For all these reasons, it the first place that any traveler should visit when arriving at a new destination.

Blessed is everyone who fears the LORD, who walks in his ways! You shall eat the fruit of the labor of your hands; you shall be blessed, and it shall be well with you. PSALM 128:1-2 ESV

It is often said there is a unique quality to the light in central Italy that makes everyone there an artist. My experiences in that region support that view. Does the soft warmth of the light in Umbria and Tuscany really have anything to do with the easy balance of work and joyful rest that is so prevalent among the people there? I don't know, but the relaxed attitude and friendly smile of this Umbrian farmer near the hill town of Orvieto suggest that he is a true artist of life. ➲

97. Dyed Yarn, Otavalo, Ecuador 98. Market Day, Ambato, Ecuador 99. Farmer, Umbria, Italy

REST & ENJOYMENT

On the seventh day God ended His work which He had done, and He rested.... God blessed the seventh day and sanctified it, because in it He rested from all His work which God had created and made. GENESIS 2:2-3

In six days God made the heavens and the earth and all that is in them. He then rested on the seventh day and was refreshed, not because He needed rest but because He was setting a pattern for Adam and Eve to follow. For six days they would work at their learning, labor, art, architecture, agriculture, evaluation, and trade, emulating God's work. Then they would rest from all their work on the seventh day, the Sabbath day, and this rest would refresh them.

Adam and Eve's first Sabbath day was actually their first full day in the world, because they were God's final creation on the sixth day. They had not worked for any of the things they were enjoying—life, food, rest, God's love and favor, the privilege of ruling for Him. Everything was a gift. What could they give Him in response when He needed nothing and had given them all they had? They could only give their heartfelt thanks and praise. On the next Sabbath they could offer the works of their hands, but even then they would simply be giving back to God what He had first given them. By resting on the Sabbath and giving thanks, they would remember their total dependence on God, the King who continually served them and cared for them.

True Sabbath rest would enable them to rule as God intended. It would inspire them to work with all their might, knowing that their labor was for God's glory; and it would also keep them from being consumed by their work, because God did not *need* it. They were free to enjoy the fruit of their hands —the wine, the bread, and the oil—and to enjoy the creation, delighting in the oceans, fields, mountains, and skies that God had made. By delighting in the world, they would imitate God, who had rejoiced as He created it (Proverbs 8:30-31). With refreshed and rested hearts, they would transform the earth with the joy of heaven.

100. School's Out! Leh, Ladakh, India

Be still, and know that I am God; I will be exalted among the nations, I will be exalted in the earth!

PSALM 46:10

Accompanying a group of surfers to the Fijian island of Tavarua to take on the legendary waves at Cloudbreak, I gained a new appreciation for the phrase "timing is everything." This job required more than perfectly timed exposures at the peak moment of action—it also had to be coordinated with the perfect timing of the surfer in catching the wave and the perfect timing of the boat driver in putting us in the perfect spot on that same wave to make the shot. That is a lot of *perfects* to bring together for ⅟₅₀₀th of a second. The most important of these *perfects,* in my mind, was that of the boat driver, who had to put us in a near vertical position on the face of a wave and then get us over the top before it broke. If we were too early, I'd miss the shot; if we were too late, I'd miss all future shots. But he did it perfectly, time after time, cresting the top and slamming down on the back side of the waves without a second to spare. On one side of the wave the surfer would shout, "Yes!" in celebration of his ride, and on the other side of the wave I'd shout, "Yes!" in celebration of catching it on dry film. ➲

101. Hikers, Berner Oberland, Switzerland 102. Los Angeles County Arboretum, California 103. Surfer, Tavarua, Fiji

There is nothing better for men than to be happy and do good while they live. That everyone may eat and drink, and find satisfaction in all his toil—this is the gift of God. ECCLESIASTES 3:12-13 NIV

☾ Impromptu celebrations, featuring joyful music and dance, are commonplace throughout the mountain cultures of the Karakoram and Hindu Kush ranges, which stretch across northern Afghanistan, Pakistan, and Kashmir.

104. Dancer, Gilgit, Pakistan 105. Hikers, Berchtesgaden, Germany

106. Ganges River, Varanasi, India

From the dawn of time, all people have been worshipers. Consciously or not, we inevitably place our trust in something—whether it is money, education, science, technology, tradition, or love; or whether it is a spouse, friend, teacher, priest, deity, or ourselves. This confident assurance is faith. We are all worshipers at heart, and the thing we trust becomes our god.

How do we explain this instinct to worship? Why are we like this? It is because we were created to worship God. Since the creation of the world, God's eternal power and divine nature have been clearly seen in all He has made, proclaiming His glory and calling us to worship Him as the Creator and Sustainer of all things. Of all earth's creatures, only man is able to consciously appreciate God's glory and praise Him for it. The animals glorify Him unconsciously, obeying Him by instinct. Man, however, was given the privilege of consciously placing his trust in God and obeying Him. Herein is the glory of man.

God gave Adam an opportunity to increase in glory by trusting and obeying Him—a command that required him to affirm that God alone is trustworthy. If he trusted in God, Adam would mature as God's image bearer. If he trusted in anything else, he would become a broken image. Because he was the father of all mankind, his choice was pivotal. It would fill the earth with either glory or brokenness.

THE GARDEN

The LORD God planted a garden eastward in Eden, and there He put the man whom He had formed. . . . A river went out of Eden to water the garden, and from there it parted and became four riverheads. GENESIS 2:8, 10

God planted a garden on the east side of Eden and filled it with beautiful trees that were good for food, including the tree of life and the tree of the knowledge of good and evil. There He placed the man He had created. This garden was far more than a fertile plot of ground; it was the special place where God would meet with Adam and Eve. God would come there and call them, and they would walk with Him and talk face-to-face.

The topography of the Garden is significant. A river flowed into it from Eden and divided into four rivers flowing down to Havilah, Cush, and Assyria, and ultimately into the sea. Because rivers flow downhill and headwaters are at the uppermost reaches of their courses, it is likely that the Garden was situated in an elevated or mountainous area, which was important to Adam and Eve's understanding of their relationship to God. From this perspective they could better appreciate the vastness of the earth and the even greater vastness of the heavens. Yes, Adam and Eve were exalted as God's image bearers, but God was infinitely more exalted. He was the Creator of all they saw, who stooped down to behold His creation. Though the highest heavens could not contain Him, He would condescend to meet with Adam and Eve in the Garden. Thus, the placement of the Garden would inspire a proper view of man and of God. "What is man that You are mindful of him, and the son of man that You visit him?" (Psalm 8:4).

107. Machu Picchu, Peru

The God who made the world and everything in it, being Lord of heaven and earth, does not live in temples made by man.

ACTS 17:24 ESV

112

Originally constructed in 1136 on what is believed to be the burial site of Muhammad's revered cousin and son-in-law, Ali, the Shrine of Hazrat Ali in Mazar-i-Sharif, is considered to be Afghanistan's most beautiful building. Destroyed by Genghis Khan but rebuilt in 1481, the shrine is home to thousands of white pigeons. A local legend says that if a gray pigeon joins the flock, it will turn white within forty days because the site is so holy. This phenomenon is more commonly attributed to the extraordinarily high levels of lime in the surrounding soil. ❧

108. Bodnath, Kathmandu, Nepal   109. Shrine of Hazrat Ali, Mazar-i-Sharif, Afghanistan

He sits enthroned above the circle of the earth, and its people are like grasshoppers.
. . . He brings princes to naught and reduces the rulers of this world to nothing.

IsaiahISAIAH 40:22-23 NIV

115

⟳ Chitral Mosque, in northern Pakistan, is dwarfed by 25,230-foot Tirich Mir, the highest mountain in the Hindu Kush range, which stands more than fifty miles away.

☊ Located on the western edge of the Tibetan Plateau, Ladakh is the last bastion of pure Tibetan Buddhist culture in the world. One of the principal monasteries here is Lamayuru, which was founded in the late tenth century and once housed up to four hundred monks.

110. Mosque and Tirich Mir Peak, Chitral, Pakistan 111. Lamayuru Gompa, Ladakh, India

Thus says the LORD: "Heaven is My throne, and earth is My footstool. Where is the house that you will build Me?" ISAIAH 66:1

🎧 Bad Shahi in Lahore, Pakistan, is one of the world's largest mosques, with a courtyard capable of holding sixty thousand people.

Perched on a hill above the 11,400-foot-high capital of Ladakh, Leh Gompa sports hundreds of prayer flags, or Lung-ta, which blow in the ever present breeze. Made in five traditional colors representing the five Buddha families and the five elements of space (blue), water (white), fire (red), air (green), and earth (yellow), the flags are printed with prayers that Buddhists believe carry blessing to all beings. ↻

The forest setting of a Shinto shrine in Nikko, Japan, is indicative of nature and ancestor worship. Chief in Shinto's pantheon of eight million gods is the sun goddess and great ancestress of the Imperial House. ↻↻

112. Bad Shahi Mosque, Lahore, Pakistan 113. Leh Gompa, Ladakh, India 114. Shinto Shrine, Nikko, Japan

THE GUARDIAN

The LORD God took the man and put him in the garden of Eden to tend and keep it. And the LORD God commanded the man, saying, "Of every tree of the garden you may freely eat; but of the tree of the knowledge of good and evil you shall not eat, for in the day that you eat of it you shall surely die." GENESIS 2:15-17

God entrusted Adam with the special task of guarding the Garden, which he would do by trusting and obeying God's commands. God gave him permission to eat freely of all the trees, including the tree of life; but God warned him to abstain from eating from the tree of the knowledge of good and evil, lest he die. If he ate from the tree of life, Adam would affirm that God was trustworthy and that Adam was willing to submit to His authority. However, if he ate from the tree of the knowledge of good and evil, Adam would be declaring that he wasn't willing to trust God, that he didn't need God for life, and that he could depend on himself for true knowledge about the world. At the heart of guarding the Garden was protecting the distinction between the Creator and the creature, between God and Adam— God was God and Adam was not.

Adam also had a responsibility to protect Eve by teaching her about the trees and leading her to worship according to God's command because Eve was created *after* God warned Adam about the tree of the knowledge of good and evil.

115. Man Praying, Swat Valley, Pakistan

There is a way that seems right to a man, but in the end it leads to death.

<small>PROVERBS 16:25 NIV</small>

↻ A Muslim pilgrim reads his Koran at the Shrine of Hazrat Ali in Afghanistan. Muslims believe that Islam's holy book is the word of Allah as revealed to Muhammad. Though it is often said that Muslims, Jews, and Christians worship the same God, the Koran expressly denies the biblical teaching that God is both personal and knowable and that He came to earth in the person of Jesus Christ, the second person of the Trinity, being fully God and fully man, to redeem people from sin and restore them to the glorious image of God.

➲ A Buddhist monk at Karsha Gompa in Zanskar, India, spins a prayer wheel and uses prayer beads to increase his merit toward attaining Nirvana, in the hope of escaping the endless chain of existence that he sees as only sorrow and suffering.

A common claim of non-Christian religions is a tolerance of other beliefs. Only Jesus, claiming to be the Son of God, said, "I am the way, the truth, and the life. No one comes to the Father except through Me" (John 14:6). His statement is not intolerant, it is simply consistent with the nature of truth—something is either true or it's not. Truth is not a value-neutral, multiple-choice option. Someday we will all have to answer the question Jesus asked His disciples in Luke 9:20, "Who do you say that I am?"

116. Shrine of Hazrat Ali, Mazar-i-Sharif, Afghanistan   117. Prayer Wheel, Karsha Gompa, Zanskar, India

Do men make their own gods?
Yes, but they are not gods!

JEREMIAH 16:20 NIV

🎧 A Hindu family in Udaipur, India, floats small oil lamps, called *diyas*, upon the waters of Lake Pichola to greet Lakshmi, the goddess of wealth, during the five-day celebration of Diwali, the annual Festival of Lights.

A ceremonial offering is carried by a Shinto priestess at Kotohira Shrine on the Japanese island of Shikoku. Long considered to be more of a Buddhist temple than a Shinto shrine, Kotohira is most revered by seafarers and pilgrims. ➲

118. Diwali Candles, Udaipur, Rajasthan, India 119. Shinto Priestess, Kotohira Shrine, Takamatsu, Japan

🎧 A Hindu pilgrim offers sunrise prayers in the Ganges River at Varanasi, India. As one of Hinduism's most sacred sites, each day Varanasi draws thousands of people who come to cleanse their souls by bathing in the waters of the Ganges, while the elderly and dying make their final pilgrimage to be cremated on the river's banks.

120. Worshipers, Pushkar, Rajasthan, India

They have no knowledge who carry about their wooden idols, and keep on praying to a god that cannot save. . . . Turn to me and be saved, all the ends of the earth! For I am God, and there is no other.

ISAIAH 45:20, 22 ESV

↻ Daily offerings of fruit and flowers are set before the Great Daibutsu in Kamakura, Japan—a forty-three-foot-high, one-hundred-twenty-ton bronze statue of Amita Buddha. Cast in 1252, the Buddha was originally housed in an enormous temple building, which was destroyed by a tidal wave in 1498.

↺ Every year on June 24 (the Southern Hemisphere's winter solstice), residents of the Andean altiplano gather at the Fortress of Sacsayhuamán, near Cuzco, Peru, to reenact the Inca ceremony of Inti Raymi. Worshipers of the sun god, Inti, whom they believed to be incarnate in the Great Inca himself, the Incas celebrated his return on this day with sacrifices and offerings such as that carried by this priestess of the sun.

121. Pilgrim in Ganges River, Varanasi, India 122. Offering, Inti Raymi, Cuzco, Peru 123. Flowers, Great Daibutsu, Kamakura, Japan

THE ATTACK

Now the serpent was more cunning than any beast of the field which the Lord God had made. And he said to the woman, "Has God indeed said, 'You shall not eat of every tree of the garden'?" GENESIS 3:1

Before creating Adam and Eve, God had created a host of angels to praise and serve Him. Satan was one of these creatures. He had been given an exalted position, but he became discontent and proud. Wanting to be God, he refused to worship and obey God, and he persuaded some other angels to rebel with him. Thus losing their glory, they desired to usurp God's glory and receive the worship of His creatures, especially His most exalted creatures, the man and the woman. Employing the serpent, the wisest of the animals, Satan attacked Adam and Eve, tempting them to trust him instead of God. Although Adam and Eve were together, Satan directed his attack at Eve. Adam's responsibility was to protect his wife, yet he failed to intervene (Genesis 3:6).

The attack was not complex. God had said that eating from the tree of the knowledge of good and evil would bring death; Satan simply contradicted God's word, saying that it would not bring death. In fact, he said, it would make the man and the woman like God, knowing good and evil. On the surface, the temptation was to trust Satan rather than God, to worship and serve a creature rather than the Creator. At a deeper level, the temptation was to worship and serve *themselves*. By trusting their own ability to judge between God's word and Satan's word, they would be setting themselves above God.

To protect Eve, Adam should have led her away from the serpent and the tree of the knowledge of good and evil and over to the tree of life. Eve's life was on the line, yet Adam, her guardian, stood by and watched as Satan tempted her. He let her eat the fruit and then ate it himself. God's image bearers were now broken images.

124. Kali Statue, Kathmandu, Nepal

You have praised the gods of silver and gold, of bronze, iron, wood and stone, which do not see, hear or understand. But the God in whose hand are your life-breath and your ways, you have not glorified. DANIEL 5:23 NASB

☾ The figure of Buddha, depicted in statues and paintings worldwide, was created by blending Greek and Indian art forms during the Kushan Dynasty (second century A.D.) in what is present day Afghanistan. For more than five hundred years prior to this, Buddha was depicted with symbols such as a wheel or footprint, but King Kanishka, wanting to emphasize the personality of the Buddha, called for a representative figure that combined the look of Greek statuary with Indian philosophical ideals.

125. *Great Daibutsu, Kamakura, Japan* 126. *Buddha's Eyes, Ladakh, India*

They exchanged the truth about God for a lie and worshiped and served the creature rather than the Creator, who is blessed forever! Amen. ROMANS 1:25 ESV

↻ A dramatic storm was clearing over the Pacific as I photographed the mysterious Moais of Easter Island. Setting up behind the statues to silhouette them against the sky and sea, I was unaware of the rainbow behind me until I turned to load a roll of film. Now totally focused on the rainbow, it took me several minutes to realize that if I ran to the other side of the Moais, the rainbow would be over their heads. It is a lesson I've never forgotten.

Chavín de Huántar, in the Andean highlands north of Lima, was home to one of Peru's oldest and least studied cultures. Evidence suggests it was a major religious pilgrimage site, where numerous animal-like deities were worshiped and ritual human sacrifice and cannibalism took place. ➲

127. Rainbow over Ahu Akivi, Easter Island 128. Chavín de Huántar, Peru

Go and cry out to the gods which you have chosen; let them deliver you in the time of your distress. Judges 10:14 NASB

How wonderful are the blessings of education, prosperity, and just government, which God has bestowed upon so many people in the world today. Yet how easy it is to trust these gifts rather than the Giver Himself, and even to believe we are independent of Him. When trials come, however, these riches cannot comfort or deliver. God alone is able.

129. University of Washington, Seattle, Washington 130. American Flag 131. Los Angeles, California

THE DEFEAT

Cursed is the ground for your sake;
in toil you shall eat of it all the days of your life.

GENESIS 3:17

Adam and Eve's rebellion was disastrous, shattering their ability to love, rule, and worship as God intended. Cursed was their relationship with each other—Adam now blamed Eve for his rebellion, and God foretold that Eve would strive against Adam's leadership. Cursed was their relationship with the creation—through painful labor Adam would bring forth food from the ground, and through painful labor Eve would bring forth children. Cursed was their relationship with God—they now hid from Him and were banished from communing with Him in the Garden. No longer able to eat from the tree of life, they would eventually die.

Every succeeding generation has been poisoned by Adam and Eve's rebellion. Our relationships with ourselves and others are marked more by blameshifting and strife than by self-sacrificing love. The creation, too, suffers the consequences of Adam and Eve's sin. From famine and earthquakes to disease and pain, the natural world appears to be at war with itself and with us. None of us seeks God, and we place our trust in created things that always fail us in the end. Finally, we die. We are broken images.

In the midst of Adam and Eve's brokenness, God offered the hope of restoration to them and to their descendants—including us. He promised that one day a descendant of Adam and Eve would crush Satan's head, though He Himself would be bruised in the process. As a sign of this promise, God killed an innocent animal and fashioned its skin into clothes for Adam and Eve to wear. This sacrifice of life would be a continual reminder of God's mercy in sparing their lives, of the consequences of trusting a creature rather than the Creator, and of the suffering the Promised One would have to endure to crush Satan, restoring Adam and Eve and their descendants to God.

132. Withered Cornfield, Arizona

The heart is deceitful above all things, and desperately sick; who can understand it?

JEREMIAH 17:9 ESV

☾ The contrast between the boldly defiant words displayed on the wall, "THE LANDS ARE OURS," and the broken spirit displayed on this woman's face is sadly ironic. It is also convicting. I photographed many such scenes during my travels before I was a Christian, and in my discomfort or lack of concern, I often used my camera as a shield to protect myself from personal involvement.

Today, however, knowing the life-changing and culture-transforming power of the love of Jesus—and knowing that poverty and injustice begin with a false view of the reality of God—I find it more difficult to hide. Or do I? The heart is deceitful indeed, and it is only by God's grace that we are aware of this.

133. "The Lands Are Ours," Quito, Ecuador 134. Otavalo Boy, Ecuador

There is none righteous, not even one; there is none who understands, there is none who seeks for God.

ROMANS 3:10-11 NASB

*Through one man sin
entered the world, and
death through sin.*

ROMANS 5:12

☾ Nowhere are the real-life consequences of
Adam and Eve's fall more disturbingly evident
than at a war cemetery. Nowhere is the truth
of God's judgment in Genesis 2:17 more
undeniably confirmed: "In the day that you eat
of it you shall surely die." Every war in history
began with the spiritual death that mankind
suffered in the Garden. The cost of the Fall was
brought home powerfully to me as I walked
among a seemingly endless sea of graves at an
American cemetery near the D-day beaches of
Normandy, France. Again and again the same
date of death appeared on the headstones: June
6, 1944. It was a day of great loss and tragedy
in the lives of thousands of families. It was also
the day I was born.

135. National Cemetery, Los Angeles, California   136. Aged Worshiper, Pashupatinath, Nepal

THE VICTORY

I will put enmity between you and the woman, and between your seed and her Seed; He shall bruise your head, and you shall bruise His heel. GENESIS 3:15

For thousands of years, God told Adam and Eve's descendants more and more about the Promised One. Faithfully worshiping God the Father, the coming Messiah would perfectly trust and obey Him (Isaiah 50). He would be the servant king Adam had failed to be and would heal man's relationship with nature (Isaiah 9, 11). He would truly love others, though they would hate Him, and He would even die to restore them to God (Isaiah 53). He would be both God and man (Isaiah 7). As a result of His suffering, God would exalt Him as King over an everlasting kingdom and would draw all nations to worship Him and call Him Mighty God and Everlasting Father. This second Adam would restore everything the first Adam had lost.

From 100 B.C. to A.D. 100, numerous Jewish men in Palestine claimed to be God's Promised One, leading their followers to revolt against the oppressive Roman government in the hope of establishing God's kingdom. But all of them were killed, imprisoned, or discredited, and their followers were scattered. One man, however, was different. His name was Jesus of Nazareth, and although He claimed to be the Promised King, the kingdom He preached was not what people expected. He said that God's kingdom would come not through armed revolt but through confessing their rebellion and turning back to God. As the people witnessed Him performing miracles, casting out demons, healing the sick and lame, perfectly loving God and man, and even claiming to be the Son of God, some were persuaded that He was indeed the Promised King. Others despised Him and, rejecting the kingdom He proclaimed, convinced the Romans to torture and crucify Him. After His death, His followers were scattered, fearing for their lives.

Soon, however, Jesus' followers were boldly declaring that He had risen from the dead with a glorious new body and He had appeared not only to them but to more than five hundred people at once. Before ascending to heaven, Jesus announced that all authority in heaven and earth had been given to Him, and He commanded His disciples to go into all the nations, baptizing them in the name of the Father, the Son, and the Holy Spirit, teaching them to obey all He had commanded. Jesus' followers, transformed by His resurrection and the power of the Holy Spirit into a fearless band of believers, now courageously spread the good news that the Promised One had come. He had defeated Satan and death, had been exalted as the King over all creation, and would grant eternal life to all who would trust and obey Him. They proclaimed His kingdom throughout the earth, and many were martyred for it. They declared that Jesus was God the Son, the true image of God, in whose image man was made and to whose image they could be restored. Those who would believe and be baptized into Jesus' body, the church, would learn to love, rule, and worship as God intended. Strengthened rather than scattered by persecution, this body of believers continues to grow today, advancing the kingdom of God as He restores men, women, and children to the glorious image of God.

143

137. Statue of Christ overlooking Yungay, Peru

At the name of Jesus every knee should bow, in heaven and on earth and under the earth, and every tongue confess that Jesus Christ is Lord, to the glory of God the Father.

PHILIPPIANS 2:10–11 ESV

↻ Having been commissioned by Jesus to disciple the nations, His followers faithfully went forth to spread the good news of His kingdom to the ends of the earth. A seventh century bishop named Cuthbert, who carried the gospel to the northernmost reaches of England, beyond Hadrian's Wall, was another such servant. Four hundred years later in 1093, a cathedral was built in Durham to house the remains of Saint Cuthbert, and it has been a principal place of worship and pilgrimage ever since. Today, Durham Cathedral is renowned as the largest and finest example of Norman architecture in all of England.

Faithful followers of Christ accompanied Spanish ships to the New World in the fifteenth century, and they brought the gospel with them. Churches such as this one in Peru's Urubamba Valley continue to pass it on. ↻

138. Durham Cathedral, England 139. Country Church, near Chincheros, Peru

God, who said, "Let light shine out of darkness," has shone in our hearts to give the light of the knowledge of the glory of God in the face of Jesus Christ.

2 Corinthians 4:6 esv

↻ With a towering 452-foot-high dome designed by Michelangelo, Saint Peter's is one of the world's most impressive cathedrals. Begun in 1443, it was not completed until 1627.

Canterbury Cathedral's Bell Harry Tower was built in the fifteenth century to replace a Norman tower that was destroyed by a fire in 1174. Before that, an Anglo-Saxon cathedral had stood here, founded by Augustine, the first archbishop of Canterbury, who was sent to England by Pope Gregory I in 597 to lead King Ethelbert and his race from the worship of idols to faith in Christ. One hundred fifty years before that, Roman Christians worshiped at this same spot. ➲

140. *Saint Peter's Cathedral, Vatican City* 141. *Bell Harry Tower Interior, Canterbury Cathedral, England*

Jesus came and spoke to them, saying, "All authority has been given to Me in heaven and on earth. Go therefore and make disciples of all the nations, baptizing them in the name of the Father and of the Son and of the Holy Spirit, teaching them to observe all things that I have commanded you; and lo, I am with you always, even to the end of the age." MATTHEW 28:18-20

142. Orléans Cathedral, France 143. The Great Commission, Saint Nicholas Cathedral, Galway, Ireland

144. Indus River, Northern Pakistan

PHOTOGRAPHIC NOTES

The following notes are for readers with an interest in photography who would like to know how the pictures in this book were made. A detailed introductory discussion of equipment and general photographic technique is provided in *The Art of God*, and a review of that information may help to better understand the more "people specific" comments that follow.

GENERAL GUIDELINES

Before addressing the techniques of photographing people, I'd like to share some guidelines that will do more for your results than anything else I might tell you. These may seem obvious, but they don't come naturally and are easier said than done. All are expressions of the second great commandment given by Jesus: "You shall love your neighbor as yourself."

• Always remind yourself that your "subject" is your neighbor—a sensitive human being.
• If the person you want to photograph is aware of your presence, ask before taking a picture.
• If you are unable to ask with words, use a smile and sign language.
• If he doesn't want his picture taken, simply thank him and move on.
• Show a genuine interest in the person, and try to learn something about him.
• Approach with your camera out of sight, and don't ask permission to take any pictures until you have connected on a human level.
• If you promise to send a print, do it. A photographer coming after you will thank you.

EQUIPMENT & TECHNIQUE

Cameras: The best camera for photographing people is small enough not to intrude between you and your subject, yet large enough to provide good quality results. Currently, this means either 35mm film or high-resolution digital equipment.

Film: Accurate color rendition of skin tones has long been a problem for film manufacturers because the saturated reds, blues, and greens that are desirable in landscape work are extremely unflattering to the human face. Great improvements have been made in recent years, however, and as of this writing I would recommend Fuji Astia (100 ASA) as the best film for producing both fully saturated landscapes and neutral skin tones.

Lenses: Although lens choice is always guided by the specifics of a particular shooting situation, these situations generally fall into two categories: close-up and personal, and environmental portraits.

Close-Up & Personal
A medium telephoto, from 85mm to 135mm, is the best lens choice for capturing powerful facial portraits. It provides the most natural-looking perspective and allows a more comfortable working distance from the subject. Shorter lenses tend to exaggerate the size of the nose, whereas longer lenses tend to exaggerate the size of the ears. But simply using the right lens will not produce a good portrait unless the lens is properly used. This means moving closer. Much closer. The single most important thing you can do to create powerful portraits is to get close to your subject. There are several reasons for this:

• Because the 35mm format is small, you must maximize it by filling the frame with only the information that is necessary. In a portrait, this means little more than head and shoulders, and to do this you must be no more than four to five feet from your subject.
• A composition this tight with a medium telephoto will be at or near its closest point of focus, which will soften the background and increase the apparent sharpness of the face.
• Moving close to your subject heightens his involvement in the picture, creating a greater intensity between you and him—and, ultimately, between him and the viewer.

Tips
• Focus on the eyes. They are the most powerful feature of the face, and their mid-plane location ensures the greatest sharpness from nose to ears.

• Use a large aperture to increase the softness of the background and decrease exposure time, thus reducing the chance of motion blur.
• If your camera has a motor winder, make a second exposure immediately after the first, as most people noticeably relax after hearing the shutter release. The second shot often captures a much more natural expression.

Environmental Portraits
A wide-angle lens, from 20mm to 28mm, is the best lens choice for environmental portraits that make a strong connection between people and their surroundings. The exaggerated perspective and increased depth of field that these lenses provide enable you to emphasize the foreground elements of a scene while directly relating them to something, or someone, in the background. As with telephoto lenses, however, it is necessary to use a wide-angle properly in order to achieve the desired results. Once again, this means moving in—closer, closer, and closer still. However, this time you are not getting close to a person, but to a foreground object related to a person. You still need to fill the frame with important information, but now you want to show more than a face. A wide angle lets you do both if you move in close to the foreground and use a small aperture to increase depth of field, so both the foreground and background elements are sharp. This technique is fully described in *The Art of God* in relation to landscape work.

Tips
• Use a vertical format for the most powerful foreground emphasis.
• Brace the camera firmly and slowly squeeze the shutter, because the small apertures required by this technique necessitate slow exposures, which can cause blurring.
• Beware of unwanted background objects, which are difficult to see when using a wide angle but easy to see in the finished picture due to the lens's increased depth of field.

PLATES

  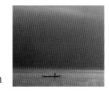 

1. *Sunset Storm, Canadian Rockies.* One of the most dramatic sunsets I have ever photographed was in Alberta's Banff National Park, when the swirling clouds of a clearing storm were set ablaze by the setting sun. Mamiya 7, 65mm lens, Velvia

2. *Sunset, Ligurian Coast, Italy.* The drama of a gathering Mediterranean storm was enhanced by using an ultra wide-angle lens and a low camera position. Pentax 645, 45mm, Astia

3. *Beach Grasses, Oregon Coast.* Wild grasses slow the encroachment of sand into Oregon's coastal communities. Linhof Technorama, Velvia

4. *Pacific Sunset, Northern California.* A telephoto lens was used to compress perspective and increase the apparent size of the setting sun off the northern California coast. Pentax 6x7, 560mm, Velvia

5. *Peacock, Los Angeles County Arboretum, California.* The brilliant colors of this peacock's feathers were intensified by strong backlighting. Olympus OM2, 100mm, Kodachrome-25

6. *Wildebeest, Ngorongoro Crater, Tanzania.* The sense of speed was accentuated by panning with the running animals while using a slow shutter speed. Topcon, 300mm, Kodachrome-64

7. *Father and Son, Chitral, Pakistan.* Shooting from an elevated pathway, I was able to simplify this composition by eliminating the horizon. Leicaflex SL2, 180mm, Kodachrome-64

8. *Sunrise, Lake Dal, Kashmir, India.* To enhance the exotic mood created by the sun rising through fog on Lake Dal, I used an 81A warming filter. Nikon F3, 80-200mm, Kodachrome-25

9. *Happy Face, Hangzhou, China.* A simple background is crucial to good people pictures. Natural spotlighting, like this from a high window, can often create a high contrast scene where the background drops out completely, focusing all attention on the subject. Canon F1, 85mm, Kodachrome-64

10. *School Children, Cereste, France.* Put two or more kids near a tourist with a camera, and silliness will usually occur. Add a motor drive, and a great picture may also occur. Pentax 645, 75mm, Astia

11. *Camel Caravan, Dunhuang, China.* Wanting to emphasize the vastness and emptiness of the desert environment, I used a telephoto lens to compress the scene and an elevated camera position to eliminate the horizon, allowing the imagination to complete the picture. Canon F1, 200mm, Kodachrome-64

12. *Sisters, Suzhou, China.* I have rarely encountered parents who didn't delight in having their children photographed, particularly in the doorway of their home, where they feel safe. Canon F1, 85mm, Kodachrome-64

13. *Merchant, Tashkurghan, Afghanistan.* Throughout southwest Asia, the bazaars offer an ideal setting for people photos, as vendors often sit in the shade and are illuminated by soft reflected light from the street. Hasselblad, 150mm, Ektachrome-64

14. *Father and Son, Ambato, Ecuador.* Few places on earth can match the intensity of color found in the markets of the Andean altiplano. Yet, its abundance is often distracting, requiring careful control of busy backgrounds. Canon F1, 80-200mm, Kodachrome-64

15. *Rajasthani Girl, Jaisalmer, Rajasthan, India.* The warmth of light in this sandstone city, on the edge of the Thar Desert, was matched by the expression of one of its younger residents. Olympus OM2, 100mm, Kodachrome-64

16. *Girl with Grandmother, Calbuco, Chile.* Once again, the security of home created a more relaxed atmosphere for this picture. Leicaflex SL2, 180mm, Kodachrome-25

17. *Prince Zia, Chitral, Pakistan.* Zia was my good friend and guide through the Hindu Kush valley of Chitral, where his family ruled prior to the creation of Pakistan. Leicaflex SL2, 135mm, Kodachrome-64

18. *Vendor, Dunhuang, China.* Close focus with a large aperture was used to accentuate the weathered character of this man's face. Nikon F3, 80-200mm, Kodachrome-64

19. *Farmer, Bamiyan Valley, Afghanistan.* The hands and sickle tell much about this farmer's life, so it was important to include them in this composition. Hasselblad, 150mm, Ektachrome-64

20. *Gun Maker, Kohat Pass, Pakistan.* Tight framing was used to add intensity to this portrait. Leicaflex SL2, 90mm, Kodachrome-64

           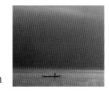       

21. Merchant, Pahalgam, Kashmir, India. The dark, out-of-focus background is crucial to the success of this composition. Nikon F3, 105mm, Kodachrome-64

22. Olive Farmer, Portugal. Selective focus (close-up with large aperture) strengthens a portrait by minimizing background distraction. Hasselblad, 150mm, Ektachrome-64

23. Altiplano Native, Cuzco, Peru. Only the information that is essential to the story you want to tell should be included in your picture. Hasselblad, 150mm, Ektachrome-64

24. Camel Herder, Pushkar, India. A tight crop was used to focus all attention on this man's face. Olympus OM2, 200mm, Kodachrome-25

25. Tyrolean Man, Hallstatt, Austria. The classic Tyrolean hat was important to include in the framing of this shot. Nikon F, 105mm, Kodachrome-25

26. Masai Warrior, Kenya. A wide-open aperture created minimum depth of focus to draw attention to the head ornament of this warrior. Hasselblad, 150mm, Ektachrome-64

27. Woman in Kimono, Miyajima, Japan. My camera position was carefully chosen to place only blue water behind the subject, focusing all attention on her face. Nikon F3, 105mm, Kodachrome-64

28. Ladakhi Woman, Leh, Ladakh, India. All the shots on this spread used tight framing and careful camera positioning to control distracting backgrounds. Olympus OM2, 100mm, Kodachrome-25

29. Folk Dancer, Segovia, Spain. A low camera position enabled me to use the sky as a seamless backdrop. Hasselblad, 80mm, Ektachrome-64

30. Rajasthani Bride, Udaipur, Rajasthan, India. Extra-tight framing greatly strengthens a portrait. Olympus OM2, 100mm, Kodachrome-64

31. Uygur Woman, Turfan, China. Indirect lighting generally yields more relaxed expressions. Nikon F3, 105mm, Kodachrome-64

32. Fishwife, Izu, Japan. Because this woman's life is lived outdoors, full sun is the best light source to convey her story. Nikon F3, 105mm, Kodachrome-64

33. Masai Woman, Kenya. A large aperture was used to soften the background. Hasselblad, 150mm, Ektachrome-64

34. Ladakhi Dancer, Leh, Ladakh, India. A low camera position allowed me to throw the distant landscape completely out of focus, drawing all attention to the dancer. Nikon F3, 80-200mm, Kodachrome-64

35. Newlyweds, Rajasthan, India. Using the plain wall of this couple's house as a backdrop simplifies the scene and adds an important informational element to the picture. Olympus OM2, 100mm, Kodachrome-64

36. Forever Young, Linz, Austria. The comfort of being in one's home makes it the ideal location for a portrait. Topcon D, 100mm, Kodachrome-25

37. Husband and Wife, Bamiyan, Afghanistan. A long lens was used from mid-distance to compress perspective and increase the apparent size of the background hills. Hasselblad, 250mm, Ektachrome-64

38. Ric and Jill Ergenbright. The photographer's slightly elevated camera position simplified the background by removing the horizon from the composition.

39. Wedding, Kamakura, Japan. A zoom lens is helpful for accurate framing when shooting from a fixed camera position. Nikon F3, 80-200mm, Kodachrome-64

40. Hindu Wedding, Rajasthan, India. Because the wedding canopy is an important feature in the Hindu ceremony, I used an extreme wide-angle lens from a very low camera position to include it in the scene. Olympus OM2, 21mm, Kodachrome-64

41. Wedding Knot, Rajasthan, India. Supporting details are crucial to telling a more complete story of any event. A long lens, combined with selective focus and a simple background, is the ideal optic for such details. Olympus OM2, 200mm, Kodachrome-64

42. Friends, Kashgar, China. The best opportunities for good pictures of children are always close to their homes, especially when they are in the safety of the doorway. Nikon F3, 80-200mm, Kodachrome-64

43. Erin, California. A shaded setting illuminated by reflected sunlight is ideal for portraits, because "bounced" light softens shadows and reduces squinting. The relaxed expressions in the pictures on this spread are a result of such lighting. Leicaflex, 60mm, Kodachrome-25

44. Apple Vendor, Ladakh, India. Olympus OM2, 100mm, Kodachrome-25

45. Sister and Little Brother, Kathmandu, Nepal. Hasselblad, 150mm, Ektachrome-64

46. Girl with Grandfather, Peshawar, Pakistan. A telephoto lens allows for a greater working distance between photographer and subject, which often produces a more relaxed expression. Leicaflex SL2, 180mm, Kodachrome-64

47. Father and Son, Chitral, Pakistan. A large aperture was used to soften the background and focus attention on the subject. Olympus OM2, 75-150mm, Kodachrome-64

154

48. Safety Zone, Ecuador. I chose to exclude the father's face from this composition to emphasize the universal "I'm safe" posture of his daughter. Had I shown his face, the picture would have been more specific in nature. Hasselblad, 150mm, Ektachrome-64

49. Kashmiri Girl, Srinagar, India. The expressive nature of hands makes them a desirable addition to any portrait, as illustrated by the pictures on this spread. Nikon F3, 80-200, Kodachrome-64

50. Festival Dress, Takamatsu, Japan. Nikon F3, 105mm, Kodachrome-25

51. Young Hiker, Kitzbühel, Austria. Hasselblad, 150mm, Ektachrome-64

52. All in the Family, Connemara, Ireland. As many of the pictures in this book show, the support of family or friends lessens the fear of being photographed—especially if one of the supporters is man's best friend. Nikon F3, Kodachrome-25

53. Friends, Otavalo, Ecuador. Common gathering places such as markets or wells are ideal settings for powerful environmental portraits. Hasselblad, 250mm, Ektachrome-64

54. Pushkar Camel Fair, Rajasthan, India. A long lens was used to compress the scene and highlight the crowded feeling of this annual event in India's Thar Desert. Olympus OM2, 200mm, Kodachrome-25

55. Portovenere, Italy. A telephoto lens flattens perspective in this scene to create a colorful architectural pattern. Tight framing further heightens the effect. V-pan 617, 360mm, Velvia

56. Taking Charge, Darjeeling, India. A motor winder was invaluable in capturing a decisive moment in this most serious discussion at the Tibetan Refugee Center in Darjeeling, India. Nikon F3, 80-200mm, Kodachrome-25

57. Manarola, Cinque Terra, Italy. The perspective-stretching ability of an ultra wide-angle lens was used to accentuate Manarola's precarious perch above the Mediterranean. Mamiya 7, 43mm, Velvia

58. Karimabad, Hunza, Pakistan. To illustrate the dominant nature of the Karakoram Himalaya in the lives of the Hunzakut people, I used a telephoto lens and a distant camera position to increase the relative size of the mountains. Nikon F3, 80-200mm, Kodachrome-64

59. Overview, Brugge, Belgium. Unusual viewpoints add interest to any subject. This shot was taken from the top of a clock tower in Brugge. Nikon F3, 80-200mm, Kodachrome-25

60. Rush Hour, Beijing, China. A high camera position combined with a low angle of light allows shadows to be used as a powerful compositional element. Nikon F3, 80-200, Kodachrome-64

61. Champs d'Elysees, Paris, France. Long exposure times of any moving light source create a colorful streak that can add visual interest to the picture. Nikon F3, 300mm, Kodachrome-25

62. Farmer, Thar Desert, India. Lying on my back to put the farmer against the huge sweep of a desert sky (the original is a vertical), I used an ultra wide-angle lens with a polarizing filter to accent the contrast between his yellow turban and the deep blue canopy above. I don't think I'd try this in the city. Olympus OM2, 21mm, Kodachrome-64

63. At the Beach, Santa Monica, California. Waves, shore birds, and kids (especially your own) consume vast amounts of film at the beach. Hasselblad, 150mm, Ektachrome-64

64. Pals, Lake Louise, Alberta, Canada. A telephoto lens allowed a distant enough shooting position to not interfere with the scene. Nikon F, 200mm, Kodachrome-25

65. Homework, Saidu Sharif, Swat, Pakistan. An elevated viewpoint draws attention to the Arabic text in the boy's book, providing valuable information to the viewer. Leicaflex SL2, 90mm, Kodachrome-64

66. *Water Works Park, Seattle, Washington.* A medium telephoto avoids interference with the subject. Pentax 6x7, 165mm, Velvia

67. *Co-op Classroom, Harbin, China.* A slightly elevated camera position creates depth by separating the front and rear students. Olympus OM2, 50mm, Kodachrome-64

68. *Professor, Beijing, China.* Tight cropping makes a more powerful picture by only showing that which is pertinent. Canon F1, 85mm, Kodachrome-64

69. *Dana and Boh, Southern California.* Using the same viewpoint as the subjects invites the viewer to join in their activity. Olympus OM2, 50mm, Kodachrome-64

70. *Working the Well, Rajasthan, India.* Selective framing and a simple background change a common scene into a graphic image of manual labor. Olympus OM2, 200mm, Kodachrome-64

71. *Fishermen, Nazaré, Portugal.* The colorful fishing boats of Nazaré return home each morning, providing unlimited photographic opportunities. Hasselblad, 250mm, Ektachrome-64

72. *Goatherd, Kashmir, India.* A high viewpoint and early morning light create a "shadow picture." Nikon F3, 80-200mm, Kodachrome-64

73. *Winnowing Grain, Bamiyan, Afghanistan.* A medium telephoto lens increased the relative size of the mountains. Hasselblad, 150mm, Ektachrome-64

74. *Plowing, Swat Valley, Pakistan.* A telephoto lens was used to emphasize the mountainous character of the land. Hasselblad, 250mm, Ektachrome-64

75. *Huaso and Sheep, Centinela, Chile.* A telephoto lens compressed the scene to emphasize the herder's rule over his sheep. Leicaflex SL2, 180mm, Kodachrome-25

76. *Winnowing, near Jodhpur, India.* A low camera position allowed the sky to be used as a seamless backdrop. Olympus OM2, 28mm, Kodachrome-64

77. *Wash Day, Udaipur, India.* Using a telephoto lens from a rowboat enabled a tight composition from a nonthreatening distance. Olympus OM2, 200mm, Kodachrome-64

78. *Picking Grapes, Turfan, China.* Filtered light beneath the grape arbor softened the contrast. Nikon F3, 80-200mm, Kodachrome-64.

79. *Sweeping, Jaisalmer, Rajasthan, India.* Tight cropping accents the pure yellow/blue color contrast in this scene. Olympus OM2, 100mm, Kodachrome-64

80. *Painter, Rumtek Monastery, Sikkim, India.* The color of this mural was heightened by tight framing. Nikon F3, 80-200mm, Kodachrome-64

81. *Navajo Jewelry, Canyon de Chelly, Arizona.* A close-up composition is often stronger than the scene that contains it. Hasselblad, 150mm, Ektachrome-64

82. *Harpist, Cuzco, Peru.* A negative background focuses all attention on the primary subject. Canon F1, 80-200mm, Kodachrome-64

83. *Peking Opera, Beijing, China.* A subject in motion is well illustrated by putting the camera on a tripod and using a slow shutter speed. Canon F1, 85mm, Kodachrome-64

84. *Flutist, Thimphu Monastery, Bhutan.* The power of this picture is due to its extremely tight framing. Nikon F3, 80-200mm, Kodachrome-64

85. *Amber Palace, near Jaipur, India.* Attracted by the repeating pattern of these golden arches, I set my camera on a tripod and waited for the right subject to pass through the scene. About an hour later, she did. Olympus OM2, 28mm, Kodachrome-25

86. *Neuschwanstein Castle, Bavaria, Germany.* See story on page 90. Pentax 6x7, 105mm, Fujichrome-100

87. *Pont du Gard, Provence, France.* An extreme wide-angle was used to take in the full sweep of the bridge and relate it to the foreground rocks. Pentax 6x7, 45mm, Fujichrome-50

88. *Great Wall, China.* The key to this shot was being there at sunrise. Nikon F3, 28mm, Kodachrome-25

89. *Roman Aqueduct, Segovia, Spain.* Moving close to the aqueduct with a wide-angle lens added depth to the scene by emphasizing its converging parallel lines. Hasselblad, 50mm, Ektachrome-64

90. *Spices, Forcalquier, France.* The close focus capability of a normal lens is useful in capturing powerful details. Mamiya 7, 65mm, Velvia

91. *Vegetable Stall, Tashkurghan, Afghanistan.* A medium telephoto allowed a nonthreatening camera position and a more relaxed expression. Hasselblad, 150mm, Ektachrome-64

92. *Produce Seller, Jodhpur, India.* Using an ultra wide-angle and a bird's-eye perspective, the clutter of the surrounding market was replaced with the seller's goods. Olympus OM2, 21mm, Kodachrome-64

93. *Grape Vendor, Peshawar, Pakistan.* A normal lens allowed a comfortable working distance, yet one that was close enough to avoid the pressing crowd in the marketplace. Hasselblad, 80mm, Ektachrome-64

94. *Frying Potatoes, Ibarra, Ecuador.* Hasselblad, 150mm, Ektachrome-64

95. *Making Bagels, Turfan, China.* An ultra wide-angle strongly emphasizes the foreground and relates it to the seller. Nikon F3, 20mm, Kodachrome-64

96. *Vegetable Seller, Jaisalmer, Rajasthan, India.* A medium telephoto was used to avoid the busy surroundings, yet not interfere with the seller's transaction. Olympus OM2, 100mm, Kodachrome-64

97. *Dyed Yarn, Otavalo, Ecuador.* The goods in a marketplace offer countless colorful details to photograph. Canon F1, 80-200mm, Kodachrome-64

98. *Market Day, Ambato, Ecuador.* An ultra wide-angle with maximum depth of field is the ideal combination for creating powerful environmental portraits. Canon F1, 17mm, Kodachrome-64

99. *Farmer, Umbria, Italy.* An elevated viewpoint eliminated the horizon and simplified this composition. Hasselblad, 150mm, Ektachrome-64

100. *School's Out! Leh, Ladakh, India.* Sitting in the landing zone, and encouraging the kids to jump into the hay, I used a motor drive to keep up with their antics. Olympus OM2, 21mm, Kodachrome-64

101. *Hikers, Berner Oberland, Switzerland.* A long lens was used to increase the relative size of the mountains. Nikon F, 105mm, Kodachrome-25

102. *Los Angeles County Arboretum, California.* A telephoto lens and a wide aperture was used to blur the flowers and freeze the child's motion. Leicaflex SL2, 180mm, Kodachrome-64

103. *Surfer, Tavarua, Fiji.* Shooting from a small boat, it was necessary to coordinate the surfer's ride with the speed of the wave and the time needed to make it over the top to safety. Canon EOS1, 35-350mm, Astia

104. *Dancer, Gilgit, Pakistan.* Olympus OM2, 75-150mm, Kodachrome-64

105. *Hikers, Berchtesgaden, Germany.* A long lens and large aperture lessen the depth-of-field to focus on the hikers. Olympus OM4, 80-200, Fujichrome-50

106. *Ganges River, Varanasi, India.* A telephoto was used with a wide-open aperture to enlarge and soften the distant sun, and increase the apparent sharpness of the silhouetted worshiper. Olympus OM4, 80-200mm, Kodachrome-64

107. *Machu Picchu, Peru.* An 81A warming filter was used to enhance the sunset light that followed a clearing storm. Canon F1, 28mm, Kodachrome-64

108. *Bodnath, Kathmandu, Nepal.* An extreme wide-angle lens and upward viewpoint emphasizes the sky and uses the flags as a leading line to the stuppa. Olympus OM4, 21mm, Kodachrome-64

109. *Shrine of Hazrat Ali, Mazar-i-Sharif, Afghanistan.* Placing my camera on the ground and clapping to launch the pigeons, I was challenged to make the exposure when the man's face was not obstructed by one of the birds. Hasselblad, 50mm, Ektachrome-64

110. *Mosque and Tirich Mir Peak, Chitral, Pakistan.* An extreme telephoto compressed the fifty-mile span of this scene and shortened the apparent distance between Tirich Mir and the mosque. Hasselblad, 500mm, Ektachrome-64

111. *Lamayuru Gompa, Ladakh, India.* A race with the sun ended with a last minute dive to the ground to steady my camera for a few shots before the sun disappeared. Olympus OM2, 200mm, Kodachrome-25

112. Bad Shahi Mosque, Lahore, Pakistan. A wide-angle was used to increase the apparent size of the mosque. Hasselblad, 50mm, Ektachrome-64

113. Leh Gompa, Ladakh, India. Shooting upward from beneath the flags placed them against a deep blue sky. Olympus OM2, 21mm, Kodachrome-25

114. Shinto Shrine, Nikko, Japan. A long lens compressed the elements of the scene to accent the shrine's animistic worship of the forest. Canon F1, 80-200mm, Kodachrome-64

115. Man Praying, Swat Valley, Pakistan. A long telephoto and foreground framing creates a feeling of privacy in this scene. Hasselblad, 250mm, Ektachrome-64

116. Shrine of Hazrat Ali, Mazar-i-Sharif, Afghanistan. Telephoto compression and tight cropping simplify the composition and strengthen its story. Hasselblad, 250mm, Ektachrome-64

117. Prayer Wheel, Karsha Gompa, Zanskar, India. A long exposure with the camera on a tripod creates a colorful blur in the moving wheel and beads. Nikon F3, 28mm, Kodachrome-64

118. Diwali Candles, Udaipur, Rajasthan, India. Looking over the shoulders of this family invites the viewer to share in their experience. Olympus OM2, 100mm, Kodachrome-64

119. Shinto Priestess, Kotohira Shrine, Takamatsu, Japan. A camera position out of the subject's line of view creates a candid feel to this image, which is enhanced by its loose framing. Nikon F3, 50mm, Kodachrome-64

120. Worshipers, Pushkar, Rajasthan, India. A camera position was chosen that drew attention to the main point of action by converging lines from all parts of the composition. Olympus OM2, 28mm, Kodachrome-64

121. Pilgrim in Ganges River, Varanasi, India. A telephoto perspective and tight cropping avoided the extreme visual clutter of Varanasi's bathing ghats. Olympus OM4, 80-200mm, Kodachrome-64

122. Offering, Inti Raymi, Cuzco, Peru. A long lens softens and simplifies the background to focus all attention on the subject. Hasselblad, 250mm, Ektachrome-64

123. Flowers, Great Daibutsu, Kamakura, Japan. Telephoto compression makes the flowers appear closer to the statue's hands than they are, and tight cropping makes a general statement about Buddhism rather than a specific comment about the Kamakura Buddha. Nikon F3, 80-200mm, Kodachrome-64

124. Kali Statue, Kathmandu, Nepal. Pigeons add necessary scale to this grotesque image of Kali. Nikon F3, 80-200mm, Kodachrome-64

125. Great Daibutsu, Kamakura, Japan. Unlike plate #123, here a wide angle lens was used from a close-up and low position to illustrate the Kamakura Buddha's height. Nikon F3, 20mm, Kodachrome-64

126. Buddha's Eyes, Ladakh, India. Specific features of the Thikse Buddha were eliminated by tight telephoto cropping to create a dramatic image of its eyes. Nikon F3, 80-200mm, Kodachrome-64

127. Rainbow over Ahu Akivi, Easter Island. See story on page 130. Leicaflex SL2, 28mm, Kodachrome-25

128. Chavín de Huántar, Peru. I used an ultra wide-angle lens at its closest point of focus to make an environmental portrait of this half human, half feline Chavín deity. Canon F1, 17mm, Kodachrome-64

129. University of Washington, Seattle. A moderate wide-angle was used to emphasize the foreground cherry blossoms without diminishing the distant campus buildings. Pentax 6x7, 75mm, Velvia

130. American Flag. A telephoto enabled tight framing while the low camera position placed the flag against the sky. Hasselblad, 250mm, Ektachrome-64

131. Los Angeles, California. A worm's-eye view is further dramatized by using an extreme wide-angle lens. Olympus OM2, 21mm, Kodachrome-25

132. Withered Cornfield, Arizona. The apparent extent of this desert wasteland was stretched by using a wide-angle lens. Hasselblad, 50mm, Ektachrome-64

133. "The Lands Are Ours," Quito, Ecuador. My framing accented the story I wanted to tell, showing this woman's despair-laden pose against the defiant words on the wall beside her. Hasselblad, 150mm, Ektachrome-64

134. *Otavalo Boy, Ecuador.* An extra-tight crop and elevated camera position heighten the emotion in this picture. Canon F1, 80-200mm, Kodachrome-64

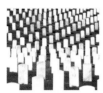

135. *National Cemetery, Los Angeles, California.* The perspective-compressing power of a telephoto lens was used to make a stronger visual statement. Topcon Super-D, 300mm, Kodachrome-64

136. *Aged Worshiper, Pashupatinath, Nepal.* A long lens was used to soften the competing background. Olympus OM4, 80-200mm, Kodachrome-64

137. *Statue of Christ overlooking Yungay, Peru.* On May 31, 1970, eighteen thousand people died when a massive landslide from Mount Huascarán buried the Andean village of Yungay. Only the cemetery, overseen by this statue of Christ, was spared. Canon F1, 17mm, Kodachrome-64

138. *Durham Cathedral, England.* A moderate wide-angle added depth to the scene by enabling the use of a foreground tree as a frame. Pentax 6x7, 75mm, Fujichrome-50

139. *Country Church, near Chincheros, Peru.* A long lens compressed the scene to emphasize the church's mountainous environment. Hasselblad, 250mm, Ektachrome-64

140. *St. Peter's Cathedral, Vatican City.* Steadying my camera on a rail to allow the use of a slow shutter speed, I exposed for the shadows, which brightened the rays as well. Hasselblad, 50mm, Ektachrome-64

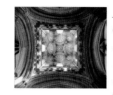

141. *Bell Harry Tower Interior, Canterbury Cathedral, England.* Shooting up into the dome provided a fresh angle that focused attention on the remarkable detail of its design. Canon EOS1, 28-80mm, Velvia

142. *Orléans Cathedral, France.* A telephoto lens was used to compress the scene and convey its dominance over the city. Nikon F, 200mm, Kodachrome-25

143. *The Great Commission, St. Nicholas Cathedral, Galway, Ireland.* Tight framing is vital in obtaining correct exposure with large stained-glass windows. Nikon F3, 80-200mm, Kodachrome-64

144. *Indus River, Northern Pakistan.* A telephoto lens was used from an elevated camera position to eliminate background elements and "flatten" perspective, emphasizing the flowing line of the riverbank. Nikon F3, 80-200mm, Kodachrome-64

145. *"Good-bye," Suzhou, China.* A distant camera position encouraged this natural response to my wave. Nikon F3, 80-200mm, Kodachrome-64

BIBLIOGRAPHY
Primary Sources

Through New Eyes: *Developing a Biblical View of the World* by James B. Jordan, ©1999, Wipf and Stock Publishers, Eugene, Oregon, ISBN 1-57910-259-X. Although there are many books that expound a *Christian* worldview, this book develops a *biblical* worldview, one that sees the Bible, the world, and man the way people in Bible times saw them. As with anything truly reformational, it will seem foreign and strange at first. Give it time. Contact: Biblical Horizons, www.biblicalhorizons.com, (800) 648-0802.

Herein Is Love: Genesis *– A Commentary for Children* by Nancy E. Ganz, ©2001, Shalom Publications, Ottawa, Ontario, ISBN 0-968830-0-1. I do not have the words to sufficiently praise Ganz's work. Through sixty-eight engaging, masterfully written lessons, she unfolds God's plan of salvation from the beginning, presenting the book of Genesis in the most powerful way I have ever read. You and your children will be incredibly blessed by her entire Herein Is Love series, as it will transform your view of the Bible and the world. Contact: Crown and Covenant Publications, www.crownandcovenant.com, (412) 241-0436.

The Original Jesus: *The Life and Vision of a Revolutionary* by Tom Wright, ©1996, Eerdmans Publishing Co., Grand Rapids, Michigan, ISBN 0-8028-4283-6.

The Challenge of Jesus: *Rediscovering Who Jesus Was and Is* by N. T. Wright, ©1999, InterVarsity Press, Downers Grove, Illinois, ISBN 0-8303-2200-3. By developing the history and the culture of Jesus' day, both *The Original Jesus* and *The Challenge of Jesus* will help you better understand Him and His message, that you might follow Him more faithfully.

Discipling Nations: *The Power of Truth to Transform Cultures* by Darrow L. Miller. YWAM Publishing, Seattle, Washington, ISBN 1-57658-015-6. This fascinating study documents how God's truth not only breaks the spiritual bonds of sin and death but can also free whole societies from deception and poverty.

How Now Shall We Live? by Charles Colson and Nancy Pearcey, ©1999, Tyndale House Publishers, Wheaton, Illinois, ISBN 0-8423-1808-9. A comprehensive, readable exposition of Christian worldview.

Additional Sources

The True Image: The Origin and Destiny of Man in Christ by Philip Edgcumbe Hughes, ©1989, Eerdmans Publishing Co., Grand Rapids, Michigan, ISBN 1-57910-285-9. Reprinted by Wipf and Stock Publishers, Eugene, Oregon. "To know and to be like Christ has from the very beginning been the destiny of man's being."

The Complete Works of Francis A. Schaeffer: A Christian Worldview, vol. 2, A Christian View of the Bible as Truth, ©1982, Crossway Books, a division of Good News Publishers, Wheaton, Illinois, ISBN 0-89107-333-7. Includes *Genesis in Space and Time* and *Art and the Bible.*

Primeval Saints: Studies in the Patriarchs of Genesis by James B. Jordan, ©2001, Canon Press, Moscow, Idaho, ISBN 1-885767-86-2. Contact: Canon Press, www.canonpress.org, (800) 488-2034.

Theses on Worship: Notes Toward the Reformation of Worship by James B. Jordan, ©1998, Transfiguration Press, Niceville, Florida, ISBN 1-883690-09-9. Contact: Biblical Horizons, www.biblicalhorizons.com, (800) 648-0802.

Foolishness to the Greeks: The Gospel and Western Culture by Lesslie Newbigin, ©1986, Eerdmans Publishing Co., Grand Rapids, Michigan, ISBN 0-8028-0176-5.

Every Thought Captive: A Study Manual for the Defense of Christian Truth by Richard L. Pratt Jr., ©1979, Presbyterian and Reformed Publishing Co., Phillipsburg, New Jersey, ISBN 0-87552-352-8.

Angels in the Architecture: A Protestant Vision for Middle Earth by Douglas Jones and Douglas Wilson, ©1998, Canon Press, Moscow, Idaho, ISBN 1-885767-40-4. A vision for culture that "embraces the fullness of Christian truth, beauty, and goodness."

Ordering Your Private World by Gordon MacDonald, ©1984, Nelson, Nashville, Tennessee, ISBN 0-8407-9549-1. MacDonald's treatment of Sabbath rest is particularly helpful.

Withhold Not Correction by Bruce A. Ray, ©1978, Presbyterian and Reformed Publishing Co., Phillipsburg, New Jersey, ISBN: 0-87552-400-1. A biblical guide for child rearing.

Reforming Marriage by Douglas Wilson, ©1995, Canon Press, Moscow, Idaho, ISBN 1-885767-34-X.

Face to Face: Meditations on Friendship and Hospitality by Steve Wilkins, ©2002, Canon Press, Moscow, Idaho, ISBN 1-59128-000-1.

RECOMMENDED BIBLICAL STUDY
Genesis 1–3

Made to Love—Psalm 139; Job 10:8-12; Acts 17:16-24; Psalm 33; 1 John 4:7-21; John 1, 17; Colossians 1:15-20.

Man—Job 38–41; Psalm 8; Hebrews 1, 2; Jeremiah 9:23-24; Psalm 16; 103; 145.

Woman—Galatians 3:26-29; Proverbs 31:10-31; 1 Corinthians 11:11-12; 1 Peter 3:3-4.

Marriage—Mark 10:1-12; Ephesians 5:21-33; Colossians 3:18-19; 1 Peter 2:22–3:8; Malachi 2:13-16; Proverbs 5:15-19; Song of Songs.

Children—Genesis 5:1-3; 17; Psalm 22:9-10; 71:5-6; 78; Exodus 20:5-6; Deuteronomy 6; 7:9-10; Ephesians 6:1-4; Colossians 3:20-21; Proverbs 3:11-12; Hebrews 12:3-11; Psalm 127, 128.

Community—Genesis 9:1-7; Leviticus 19:9-18; Romans 13:8-10; Luke 10:25-37; 1 John 4:7-21; 1 Corinthians 12; Romans 12:3-8; James 3:6-12; Psalm 67.

Made to Rule—Psalm 136; 145; 147; Genesis 8:20–9:3; Psalm 8; Mark 10:35-45; Philippians 2:1-11.

Learning—Psalm 19; 36:9; 94:9-12; Proverbs 1:1-7; 6:6-11; 30:18-31; Job 39; 1 Kings 4:29-34; Isaiah 40:12-31.

Labor—Proverbs 31:10-31; Psalm 104; Proverbs 6:9-11; 12:11; 14:23; 1 Thessalonians 4:9-12; 2 Thessalonians 3:6-12.

Art & Architecture—Proverbs 8:22-31; Exodus 25-28; 31:1-11; 35:4–39:43; 1 Chronicles 15:16-29; 2 Chronicles 3, 4; Genesis 4:17-22; Psalm 149, 150; 102:25-28; 127:1; Revelation 21:9-21; Luke 6:46-49.

Evaluation & Trade—Genesis 4:3-7; Hebrews 11:4; Matthew 25:14-30; 1 Peter 2:18; Ephesians 4:28; 6:5-9; Colossians 3:22–4:1; Leviticus 19:35-36; Job 31:13-23; Exodus 22:25-27; 1 Timothy 6:17-19.

Rest & Enjoyment—Exodus 20:8-11; 31:12-17; Deuteronomy 5:12-15; Mark 2:23-28; Isaiah 58:13-14; 1 Chronicles 29:1-22; James 1:17-18; 1 Thessalonians 5:18; Psalm 127:2; Luke 12:13-34; Ecclesiastes.

Made to Worship—Matthew 6:19-24; Psalm 115; 135; John 3:27; Revelation 4:11; Proverbs 16:25; Job 12; Daniel 2; John 14:15, 21-24; 1 John 2:3-5; 5:3; James 2:14-26; Luke 6:43-45.

The Garden—Ezekiel 28:13; 2 Chronicles 6, 7; Isaiah 66:1-2; Acts 7:55-56; Ezekiel 1:1; Revelation 4; Matthew 3:16-17; Acts 1:9-11; Mark 16:19; Luke 24:50-51; 2 Kings 2:1-11; Matthew 6:10.

The Guardian—Revelation 5:11-14; 9:1-11; 12; 20; Job 1:6-12; 2:1-10; 2 Peter 2:4; Jude 6; Matthew 25:31-46; Mark 5:1-20.

The Attack—John 8:39-47; Ephesians 6:10-20; 1 Peter 5:8-9; Proverbs 1:7; 3:5-7; 4:23; 11:2; 28:26; James 4:6-8; Isaiah 44:9-20; 46; Jeremiah 10:1-16.

The Defeat—Romans 8:19-22; Psalm 14:1-3; Titus 3:3; Romans 1:18–3:23; Proverbs 20:9; 1 John 1:8; Ecclesiastes 7:20; 9:3; Ezekiel 18:4; Leviticus 1:1–6:7; Hebrews 9:11–10:18.

The Victory—Isaiah 9:1-7; 11; 50-53; 61; Ezekiel 36–37; Daniel 7:9-14; Luke 1–4; Mark 14:53-65; John 5; 18; 19; Luke 24; Acts 1–4; Hebrews 1–2; 1 Corinthians 15; 2 Corinthians 2:12–4:6; Ephesians 1; Colossians 1:15-23; Revelation 5; 7:9-17; 21-22.

145. *"Good-bye," Suzhou, China*   Prints from this book are available at www.artofGod.com